From Failure to Promise

From Failure to Promise
- "360 Degrees" -

DR. C. MOORER

ISBN: 978-1-48405079-8 (sc)

Library of Congress Cataloging-in-Publication Data

Printed in the United States of America

Dedication

In loving memory of my father, Mr. Cleamon Moorer, Sr.,
for teaching me how to walk in faith and not to stop on the
hill, but to go all the way to the mountaintop.

Acknowledgments

I am grateful for my wife, Nicole. She is truly the support system that keeps my drive for excellence in motion. She's walked with me from and through the valley and provided light and encouragement during the darkest moments.

We are blessed to be the parents of four children, Cleamon III, Cleshaun Nicholas, Christian Clevon, and Colomon Levi. My desire to create a legacy and to live a life of great promise before them has driven me beyond many limitations.

I appreciate the tireless efforts of my mother, Mrs. Dorris Jean Moorer, for giving me love, life, nourishment, care, and support from birth to adolescence.

This book wouldn't have become a reality without all of the many talented and supportive family members, friends, colleagues, and acquaintances who helped me along the way to reach promise.

I also would like to recognize many of my adversaries for their inadvertent encouragement that made me seek God and grow closer to Him at every pivotal point in my life.

Most importantly, I thank God the Father for all things and for allowing me the opportunity to share this story of how His grace and favor transformed my life.

Contents

Foreword

"Good Morning! Good Morning!" The energetic greeting queued frantic attempts to discontinue all morning delicacies. Music was paused on smartphones, Facebook was minimized on tablets, whole bagels were devoured in milliseconds, and all attention was granted to the room's, latest entrant.

His name was Dr. Cleamon Moorer, Jr., but we called him Dr. C. and he walked into our Organizational Development (OD) class with enough passion and zeal to feed a community of lethargics and passives. It was 9 o'clock AM on a Saturday morning during Chicago's fall season, so we exhibited the symptoms of passiveness. Lucky for us, the proverbial cure was standing before us and cold Saturday mornings is where engaging and knowledge-infused afternoons met.

So when our OD class ended, my communication with Dr. C. did not. When I became a healthcare consultant, I tapped Dr. C. for advice. While working on my debut novel, Karma's Heartbeat, I tapped Dr. C. for advice. So when Dr. C. tapped me to write the foreword to his follow-up novel, From Failure to Promise: 360-Degrees, I was a mile and a city block beyond honored.

From Failure to Promise: 360 Degrees, a continuation of From Failure to Promise: An Uncommon Path to Professoriate, does the world an extraordinary service in opening our eyes to other complexions of thought, different hues of progression and an aroma of triumph that encourages collective fist pumps and uninterrupted rounds of applause.

We connect with the west-side of Detroit native on a cellular-level as he takes us to the epicenter of his past failures, his brave "360-degree" revisit and the arrival of promise in the space failure once occupied. We see him as a former college flunk out, college graduate, college professor and philanthropist. We see Dr. C. as a family man and friend; a scholar and change agent; and as a creative thinker and progressive. From Failure to Promise: 360 Degrees shows how promise begets providence in the realm of unrelenting perseverance and altruism.

Jason Henderson - Mentee and Former Student

Day of Promise

I can do all things through Christ who strengthens me!

– Philippians 4:13 NIV

Weeks one, two, and three had all gone by rather slowly following the most character-defining job interview of my life. Those weeks seemed like months, filled with hope, courage, reflection, and anxiety. You see, I prayed and applied for a teaching position at Dominican University seven years ago, to what appeared to be no avail. Even though I've been a university professor for several years now, my hope of having a desirable tenure-track position at a college or university of my aspiration had gone amiss so far.

I apologize. I'm moving a little too fast... the cover of this book does say "failure." Ask yourself: can a college "flunk-out" become a university professor? To ask it differently, can someone of the lowest ranks or classes reach the highest echelon of academic achievement? In this book, I intend to tell the story of how God used my determination and obedience to propel me from failure to promise. Promise comes from within; it has to be harnessed, cultivated, manifested, and then realized. You see, many of our beginnings do not always indicate great promise.

I'm from Detroit, Michigan, where I attended Detroit Public Schools in the 80s and early 90s. I grew up in the crime-ridden inner city. I would become the first college-bound person in my nuclear family, with what appeared to be no sound way of financing my dream education in engineering at GMI Engineering and Management Institute.

By the way, four years at one of the city's magnet high schools did not prepare me nearly enough academically or socially for GMI. Many of you may already have guessed what happened a term or two into my first year at the college. I once again must place emphasis on the fact that I became a "flunk-out" in contrast to a "drop-out".

Many dropouts may lack faith early or face what seem to be insurmountable circumstances, and they determine that either they can't get it or that they don't want to get it considering what it would cost physically or economically to continue their education. We, the conquerors, undergo a series of setbacks only to be set up for the promise that God has in store for us.

For a flunkout, promise can be deemed unattainable when the student incurs a series of failing grades, a deplorable transcript, and multiple layers of financial debt from his/her unfulfilled attempts at earning credit hours. All of those factors can lead to a letter of academic dismissal from the university's provost, followed by a notification that the student's letter of appeal was denied by the institution's academic review committee.

This flunkout passionately, wanted to graduate and to become an engineer, but initially failed to achieve academic success. However, I also failed to quit. I wanted it so badly that I refused to give up! This drive required me to change my mental, physical, and spiritual habitat in order to enable positive forces and people around me to assist me in visualizing and ultimately attaining promise. I had to put God first in all of my pursuits. I also had to focus all of my energies and talents on the pursuit of positive endeavors.

I carried my past record of failure and inadequate preparation into early adulthood. However, I continued to pursue my education, and I went on to become an engineer and global service executive at the world's leading telecommunications company.

Leaving corporate America to pursue a career in academia initiated growth, self-discovery, opposition, bias, service, joy, and triumph. Even after completing a doctorate of business administration (DBA) and earning the rank and title of doctor, I believe that my great promise continues to intrigue my thoughts and drive my ambitions.

As for now, as you must have guessed, I am a university professor. I pray that through this story, many of you will see and understand how your pasts, your current situations, or predicaments do not prevent you from reaching a desirable destiny. Many of your experiences and circumstances prepare you for a future of promise.

Now back to my earlier note of apology for getting off to such a quick start, I was on the brink of sharing with you some of the events of my life-changing "day of promise"--- December 7, 2009. This was day twenty since my interview at Dominican University. I was at home when my cell-phone rang at about 3:30PM, and I noticed it was a familiar number. "Dr. Clem Moorer speaking," I said.

"Hello Clem, this is Arvid Johnson, Dean of the Brennan School of Business at Dominican University; how are you?" My heart skipped beats as I replied, "Arvid, I'm great today...and yourself?"

"Well, I'm just fine... I'm calling you to make you an offer to join us as a tenure-track assistant professor of management in the Brennan School of Business. Clem, how do I tell you? Faculty members are still talking about your teaching demonstration, your scholarship and track record of publications are superb, and I know that you will be an excellent fit for our university and the Brennan School of Business. I apologize, if I am rambling... but I see you've been at a few universities, and I know that not only will you transform us, but we will also transform you, by making this a home for you. Will you please join me in making the Brennan School of Business one of the greatest business schools in the world?"

I replied, "Arvid, yes I will. This is the moment that I have been working toward and awaiting my whole life."

My heart was filled with joy. As Psalm 118 reminds us and the hymnist sings: *"This was indeed the day that the Lord has made, and I will rejoice and be glad in it, this is the day, this is the day, this is the day that Lord has made...."*

Throughout this book, I will share with you many of the experiences, trials, and tribulations that led up to this day of promise. Most of the experiences described will be reinforced with biblical passages to demonstrate and validate that God the Father orchestrated my journey. In addition, as you read and reflect on your own life, you will be equipped with many of the necessary tools and learn to read the signposts for charting your path. My hope is that you will also gain the assurance that even through failure, you are indeed on the path that God has set for you.

Friends and believers please take this chronological journey with me, *From Failure to Promise: 360 Degrees.*

Chapter 1 – It Began With Hope

Be strong and take heart, all you who hope in the LORD.

— Psalm 31:24

1985

Mr. Sumner served as Parker Elementary school's social studies teacher and director of the drama club. My entry into the drama club happened indirectly. In grade school and middle school, I was quite the troublemaker. My mischief consisted of acting out in class, throwing spitballs, fighting; plain-old "insubordinate" sums it up. On an unusual occasion, my fourth grade teacher, Mrs. Daniels, decided not to send me to the principal's office for my latest episode of misconduct. Instead, she escorted me to Mr. Sumner's fifth grade social studies class. He made me sit quietly in the corner and take notes during his lecture.

During the second half of lunchtime, the drama club, consisting of fourth and fifth graders, came into Mr. Sumner's classroom to practice their lines for an upcoming production. Mrs. Daniels obviously forgot to return to get me in enough time to join my class for lunch. I never knew that our school had a drama club. Instead of being sent to the principal's office as usual, I now experienced a form of punishment that exposed me to what I could have been doing only if I'd learned to behave in class.

The students were going back and forth, reading lines from a script. Midway through their rehearsal, Mr. Sumner asked me, "Do you think

5

you can read this script, where it says Anansi?" I grudgingly replied, "*I guess,*" coupled with an unconcerned shrug. I began to read the script while paying close attention to how the other students were reading. They read with enthusiasm and spark as though the storyline was alive and as if the characters were actually real. I smiled for the first time in a long time, because my antics, personality, thick glasses, and humor were what amused the other kids. Laughter was usually a result of the scolding brought on by my misbehavior.

I returned to Mrs. Daniel's class later that day from my intervention. I didn't have the usual headache that I incurred from crying in the principal's office. "Did you get suspended again," asked one of the blameless teacher's pets. "Nope, I'm going to be in one of the school plays; you just watch," I replied. A sense of determination to do more than ride my bike or watch '*He-Man*' after school filled my mind from that afternoon and for several weeks following. As I day-dreamed the rest of the class period away the unmistakable sound of the dismissal bell rang. The clamor of lockers slamming, running students, and the roar of homeroom teachers bringing order to the hall disturbed my solace. "Clear your desks; rows one and two line up first by the door quietly," Mrs. Daniels commanded. No guess or question at all about what it was time to do.

My home-life, unlike my school-life, was good. I was only reluctant about returning home from school when either I had a note stapled to the back of my shirt or fear of an impending phone call from one of my teachers to report my latest mischief of the day. "Did you get into trouble today," asked mom. "Yes Momma, I did, but I'm in the drama club now, if it is okay with you and Daddy." Instead of discussing what I did wrong in Mrs. Daniel's class that day, I was much more excited about my first day reading with the drama club. My mother sighed and said, "We'll see." I did not like to disappoint my parents, but in hindsight, disappointment was the by-product of my misbehavior, not the intended result.

My mother was always home to greet me on the days that she did not pick me up from school. She was a stay-at-home mom. She was also my father's partner in the business. My parents owned an auto repair shop properly titled 'C&M Collision'.

As I remember it briefly explained, Momma did the paper work but Daddy made the paper. And there was my older brother Julian. We're four years apart. To my parents' good luck, he didn't have any behavior problems in school. We grew up on the west-side of Detroit on a very busy street in a lower-middle-class neighborhood. There were several two-parent homes in my neighborhood. Most if not all the fathers worked. On Sunday mornings, you could see a couple of other families on our block heading off to church.

Our neighborhood was very decent. Drug-trafficking and gang violence became very prevalent in Detroit in the 1980s. We were slightly removed from many of the detriments but not immune to them. Julian and I enjoyed playing outside with the kids who lived next door. Doing chores, going to church, and vacationing on family trips to visit our grandparents, aunts, uncles, and cousins fills my mind as I reflect upon childhood.

As I explain my beginnings and how I grew up, I want to place emphasis on school. Most of my enjoyment stemmed from academic and extracurricular activities. I enjoyed sports, playing outside in the neighborhood, wrestling Julian, and visiting my cousins. However, it was always more fun for me to be learning something or demonstrating my learning.

The moment of truth for my learning and memorization came in April of 1985. "Is it really necessary for the lights to be that bright?" I was full of questions and anxiety on the opening night of our new production titled "Parker Players Presents: A Night to Remember". After several months of practicing, memorizing lines and tireless rehearsals, the big night had finally come. We were performing four plays {Anansi & Bug, The Amazing Benjamin Banneker, The Deadly Cobra, and Six Hard-Boiled Eggs} from 6:00PM to 10:00PM in the school's auditorium.

I had a leading or supporting role in each of the plays. I never gave too much thought pertaining to how, or if, I would remember lines. However, I definitely *hoped* to remember them and didn't want to get any of my roles confused.

In the end, I was able to recall all of my lines and had fun in character on stage, while even whispering some of the lines to my fellow cast members. In the dim of the auditorium, I could see my parents on the front row.

Teachers, administrators, parents, siblings, aunts and uncles, and hosts of other people from the community filled the auditorium. I felt like the night was mine; but at the age of ten, I recognized that God helped me to memorize all of those lines. This was truly the first time in my life that I realized that God helped me. Sure, I got baptized at age seven but I didn't truly know what any of it meant in the bigger scheme of things. We attended Sunday school and morning service each week. Like many children and some adults today, for most of my life, I viewed church and school as separate until after the performance.

I couldn't believe that all of our months of preparation had actually paid off. It was 10:15PM and I was still wired-up. My parents gave me a big hug, and I ran off to the dressing room to change clothes. I pondered the thoughts of God showing up and sticking around for all four plays to help me remember all of my lines.

1987

Child-stardom wasn't next for me. I continued on in the drama club for a couple of years after leaving Parker. Mr. Sumner changed the name of the drama club from the Parker Players to the "Young Performers of Detroit." We rehearsed and performed plays out of the basement of a local church. Acting was a pastime for me. At that juncture, my mind was on going to middle school.

Most of the kids in the neighborhood attended Charles R. Drew Middle School (Drew). Drew was a school with a reputation ('bad rep'). I recall several of my grade school administrators giving me a forewarning which often started with "Wait until you get to Drew…!" I knew that Julian survived it, and I hoped that he paved the way for me. In addition, I felt good knowing that a lot of my friends from Parker and kids from my block would be there also.

My advanced standing and placement got me into the "accelerated" home-room 6-16. For the sake of reference, six stood for sixth grade and

16 for Room 16. Our homeroom teacher, Mrs. Buchner, was bold and straight-forward. She shared with us that she didn't teach for money. Mrs. Buchner dressed really nicely and drove a convertible Mercedes Benz. As kids, we thought she was rich. She told us that she worked for the love of education. She also explained that her home-room students are always held in the highest regard around the school, and she would come to our defense in any situation involving another teacher. Her exact words were, "Everybody knows that I don't play!"

The accelerated class, by title alone, indicated separatism. I knew I would be in for struggles for a number of reasons. First, I was a nerd in the fullest sense of the word. I liked to learn, learned quicker than most, and had the glasses and physical frame that embodied it. Secondly, I was proud to be a nerd; never did I think that "nerdiness" meant second-class citizenship. Third, only one of my buddies from Parker was in the accelerated-class with me. Fourth, of course the class was predominantly made up of girls; and what 11-13 year old boy wouldn't want to be in a class full of pretty and smart girls?

When not distracted, I excelled in all of my subjects. I enjoyed science and math the most and I especially liked academic games. Misbehavior was once again my biggest problem. I got bored easily in school and I didn't feel handsome. Lanky arms, a big-head, and a serious set of glasses were my distinguishing attributes. These insecurities and an untapped capacity to excelled to fighting, arguing, and other disruptive behaviors. Three-day and sometimes five-day suspensions from school were a commonplace.

My mother tried to make sense of my behavior and would give me spankings. I once made the mistake of having an ill-advised conversation with one of my friends on the block about whippings. Kids often compare everything, from Christmas gifts, to family trips, to whippings. "Whose whippings hurt the most, your Momma's or your Daddy's?" I replied with great confidence, "My Daddy's, because my Momma's whippings don't even hurt that bad…" Thus, the very next time, Mom disciplined me, the story-line went like: "So my whippings don't hurt, huh?"

Terrifyingly, I'm sure many of you can imagine what ensued for the next 15 minutes or so.

Dad was of few words at the brink of discipline; he saved his energy for facilitating the intervention. On a serious note, my brother and I were not abused; we were loved, nourished, and chastised. Our parents had a way of letting life teach us some of the most important lessons.

One of which was getting kicked out of the accelerated-class due to the number of suspensions incurred between sixth and seventh grade. In fact, it was four of us altogether who got transferred out; myself, Aarmon, Michael, and Tyrone. We were now a part of homeroom 8-132. Ms. McGhee welcomed us and we blended with the other students eventually.

During the first week in the new homeroom, I remember a kid saying, "…you must not be that smart, because you were not smart enough to act right"! He was correct. In my displacement, I learned that behavior is just as important as academic intelligence; and true intelligence begins with learning how to behave with dignity, respect, courtesy, civility, and compassion.

1990

Now that misbehavior wasn't an issue any more, Ms. Wilson, one of the school's guidance counselors, talked to me and my mother about alternatives to the neighborhood high school and the possibility of getting into one of the magnet programs. Ms. Wilson frankly told me during some of my last few months of eighth grade, "Cleamon, I would hate to see you waste your talent; you can be anything in this world, if you push for it."
Those words stuck with me. I envisioned myself making the commute from the neighborhood each day to one of the city's magnet high schools.

Cass Technical High School, Martin Luther King Jr. Senior High School, and Renaissance High School were Detroit's top schools in terms of academic performance. Alumni of all three often argue about the pecking order of the schools and their programs. I list them in alphabetical order when discussing them. The city's most high-achieving and highly-connected middle school students were given the opportunity to test to get into the schools.

Students were asked to give their preference and wait for the results to come in the mail. I hoped to get into one of those schools. Weeks later, the letter that we all awaited finally came in the mail. My mother opened it and began to read aloud:

"To the parents of Cleamon Moorer

We regret to inform you that Cleamon's performance on the entrance exam does not warrant admission at this time..."

I could see that she was terribly disappointed and was in disbelief. I, on the other hand, questioned whether my record of suspensions and misbehavior for the last several years posed a red flag to decision makers. "I'm better off; those schools are all too far away anyway; plus all of my friends will be going to Mackenzie," I thought. However, in my heart I still hoped to get into one of the better schools.

Sustain me according to your promise, and I will live; do not let my hopes be dashed.

— Psalm 119:116

As I reexamine my growth and early development, this is the type of disappointment that I needed in the beginning of my journey. *Hope* alone doesn't yield results. In life, we sometimes negate the advantage and possibilities of higher aptitudes if we're initially faced with disappointment or rejection. Weeks had followed and the school year was winding down, when another letter came in the mail. This letter was sent from Dr. Martin Luther King, Jr., Senior High School...

"To the parents of Cleamon Moorer

We are pleased to inform you that after careful consideration of Cleamon's academic performance we would like to offer him admission into our Center for International Studies and Commerce (CISC) program here at M.L. King HS..."

My mother called the shop to read my dad the letter. "Honey," mom shouted. "Guess what, Pumpkin has gotten accepted into Martin Luther King High!"

Dad rarely expressed great excitement. He replied, "Well, you haven't seen anything yet, just learn to wait on the Lord, and He will see you through." "Now here God is again," I thought to myself.

Was He around when I got the rejection letter? How about when I got kicked out of the accelerated-class? The bad things that happened before didn't matter that much to me anymore. I was consumed with joy and excited about the good news. Solid academic programs come with a huge adjustment and committment.

The CISC program was no joke. My commute to King started around 6:00AM, and I was usually back at home around 6:00PM. We were required to take two foreign languages for all four years, plenty of math, science, and literary arts. Most of these courses were taught at an AP level.

I skated through the first semester with dismal scores. Mainly, because I couldn't help but wonder if my friends at Mackenzie had an easier workload. It wasn't just the comparisons of the schools that bothered me. I felt the exhaustion of my commutes and the challenge of actually studying difficult subjects every night.

I ran into one of my best friends from middle-school, LaJuan, during one of our city-wide ROTC exhibitions. He was the coolest guy in the accelerated class at Drew. Juan lived two streets over from me and on weekends our mothers would often drop us off downtown at the arcades. I was really glad to see him. I yelled to the top of my lungs in the lobby, "What's up Juan?" He responded, "Cle, my man, what's up?"

We began to exchange experiences pertaining to our different schools and programs. LaJuan led the conversation by saying, "Man, the Mack (Mackenzie) is all good; I'm banging out a 4.0; I'm in AP everything; I'm still close to home; and all of our homies and the females from Drew are there. But what's up with King?" I knew I could always keep it real with Juan and tell him how I felt, so with no hesitation I responded, "I'm getting banged at

King! Dude, some days when I don't get dropped off, I end up taking two or three buses. I leave out when it's dark and get back home when it's dark out. I'm trying to learn Chinese and French, on top of all that, dude my GPA is about a 2.5…" Being the good friend that Juan was, he reminded me that Mackenzie was my neighborhood high school and all I had to do was request a transfer. "Cle, we'll be back together again, A-cing everything and clowning."

Once again, I felt another timely and well needed intervention. God had shown up again, even at an ROTC exhibition; because who would've thought that I would run into Juan, and get put back on track? So my path and work were set before me. I had to convince my parents that King and the CISC program was way too hard; and I could reach the same if not better results by transferring to Mackenzie. My 'C-' GPA spoke for itself.

I pleaded my case to my mother. Like most good mothers, she couldn't stand to see one of her children in distress. She called the guidance counselor for AP students at Mackenzie. He explained, "If Cleamon is at King, he should stay there. Yes, we do have an AP program, but I believe he is far better off. However, we cannot deny him, because this is his neighborhood school."

She left the decision up to me, with the only contingency of talking it over with my father first. I called Dad at the shop to present my case. "Daddy, Momma said it's up to me and you." He asked, "Which one will be better for you in the future?" "They'll probably be just about the same," I replied. "No, you want to be an engineer and get into a good college," he was just warming up.

"Nope, you might as well fix it in your mind that you are going to do good and stay out there at King every day. See, the good things in life come with sacrifice, sweat, tears, hard work; you might even have to bleed a little. Everything will be alright if you buckle down and get it done, and don't cry like a little sissy every time something doesn't go your way. I'll see you when I get home, and we'll talk more. Let me talk back to your Momma…"

I was broken, and solemnly responded, "Yes sir, here she is…"I don't know what else they spoke about pertaining to the matter. However, I knew that he was done talking to me about it. "Daddy didn't even finish the third grade and he runs his own business. How is he going to tell me what's best for the future?" Could it be that he wanted so much better for me, as God wants the best for all of his children?

"For my thoughts are not your thoughts, neither are your ways my ways," declares the LORD. As the heavens are higher than the earth, so are my ways higher than your ways and my thoughts than your thoughts.

— Isaiah 55:8-9

By 11th grade, I had still not found a way to increase my GPA. However, I was learning a great deal. Julian had just left to go to the Army earlier in the year. My parents made it clear to me that I would have some decisions to make soon. The first report card marking of the year, I got my usual 2.66 GPA. I went to the shop to show it to my father.

This is a day that I will never forget. "You ain't showing me nothing!" Then he tossed the report card across the desk as if it were a sales receipt for penny candy. I asked, "What do you mean?" Angrily he responded, "It's not your best, more of the Bs and Cs should be As; and, I'm supposed to get you a car, huh, you ain't showing me nothing." I was determined that he wouldn't throw another report card at me again. In fact, I vowed, "The next report card I get, he will be putting it up on the wall in a frame."

The returning of homework assignments has the same positive, negative, or neutral effect on most. In our math class, I waited hesitantly for the return of my usual C-/D+ papers. This wasn't the norm for many of the students in our class. There were a couple of kids who seemed to 'A'-ce everything.

The Principal had a 4.0 club; which I never imagined being a member of. In fact, it was all girls in the club except for two boys. One of the boys in the club was also in my math class. Amos was a senior, and he had been in the club for years. Above all, he was headed off to Morehouse College the following year. "Amos, thanks for helping with my homework, I'll call you tonight..." This was a usual pleasantry and salutation for him. All the students in the class would gather around Amos for help, tutoring, and instruction on algebra and trigonometry.

"So girls just call you up and get help with their homework", I asked. "*Yes*, I like math," he replied. I boldly demanded to know, "But how do you get As in everything?" He began to explain that he works hard and starts studying as soon as he gets home from school, takes a break, talks on the phone and then studies again. He reiterated, "I like to be ahead of what the teacher will be teaching the next day, so that I can already have the work done and be able to answer questions instead of asking so many questions."

I thought, "*that's it!*" Studying was the last thing that I did each night before going to bed. Some kids do twice as well because they put in twice the work. "What would happen if I started putting in three-times the work?"

I took the time to revisit my earlier thoughts pertaining to "nerdiness". One of my favorite sitcoms growing up was called, *'A Different World'*. The main character of the show, 'Dwayne-Wayne', portrayed by Kadeem Hardisson, embodied total nerdiness by most people's standard. However, he achieved greatness and gained great popularity as he went from college student to engineer and then to professor. Amos and Kadeem had a great impact on my thinking at a very pivotal time in my development. Nerdiness can convert to coolness, as long as you work on the social ineptness portion of the phenomenon...I concluded. By the second report card marking of junior year, I earned nothing less than a 3.86. I became a repeat member of the Principal's 4.0 club and I inspired and motivated some of my friends to start studying more and being all that they could be.

My climb in class ranking made me a candidate for the National Honor's Society. One of the greatest joys came when my parents came to parent-teacher conference and found that their attendance was simply a formality. I began to understand that if I began with hope, and if I pushed harder and believed God, I could accomplish anything. Things don't always start off the way that they end.

> *For everything that was written in the past was written to teach us, so that through endurance and the encouragement of the Scriptures we might have hope.*

> – Romans 15:4

Take a moment to visit or revisit some of your hopes. Do some of your hopes seem unattainable? Are or were there seemingly insurmountable obstacles facing you in the pursuit of your dreams? Did you set out on the path of goal attainment and run into adversity? Your answers to these questions will help determine your attitude and aptitude as you plan to take the path set before you.

Throughout the rest of this book, I want to share more precise experiences, scripture, and interventions of trial and triumph as God navigated and orchestrated me around, over, and through obstacles on my path to promise.

Chapter 2 – The Plan to Achieve

1992

The first taste of success brought pleasant smells and feelings to my sensory channels. I wanted to keep it going and live in the moment forever. Mom said, "We are so proud of you that we don't know what to do," as we rode down the Interstate leaving parent-teacher conference. The highway was often the quickest way to travel from the west side of Detroit to the east side. My eyes followed the signs as usual counting the stops to our exit. This spring afternoon was far from typical for us. We were together as a family in the family's 'Sunday go to meeting' car in the middle of the week. Dad closed the shop just for this conference.

I remember wishing that he could have more days off to do whatever he wanted to do. However, knowing that we could sit and talk early in the day on that particular afternoon was good enough for me. We rarely sat down for dinner as a family growing up. My parents usually ate dinner in their bedroom while watching television. I sat down at the kitchen table most evenings for dinner. Before Julian went to the army, he would join me at the table.

So, when I wanted to have that evening chat with my parents, I would knock on their bedroom door and stand in the doorway to communicate with them. Dad would come into the living room to talk to me after dinner when it was really important. "This report card is going up on the wall in my office… I knew you had it in you," dad said. "It feels good and I just want to keep it going," I said. I felt that since I achieved excellence, I could do it again.

However, I feared the unknown in terms of what will happen when it gets more difficult. It has to get harder than high school. I planned to offset my fear about the next level by proclaiming success in all I attempted from that point on. In review of getting the 4.0 for the first time, I felt different and even subconsciously I may've begun to act differently. Not too differently; I was still recognizably an inner-city Detroiter. As a teen, you begin to take more consideration of the style and "flavor" of your home-town. Having cousins visit from out of town often serves as a reminder of differences in cities and even regions, for that matter.

I couldn't keep up with the latest trends and really didn't have a desire to do so. Denim jean outfits, team-logo jerseys, polo-shirts, and Michael Jordan sneakers were the staples in a well-dressed urban boy's closet. As for me, I really didn't get off into wearing or broadcasting someone else's name across my feet or back. I respected Michael Jordan's incomparable play on the basketball court, but I didn't want to put his name all over my back, because that is his last name and mine is *"Moorer."*

I really started thinking about the future. The trendiness of the day's fashion wouldn't carry over into the months ahead. How you look and dress can motivate you, and it can also motivate others to act and think favorably or unfavorably of you.

I wanted to be timeless in appearance and style. There is something about a nice pair of slacks, a starched shirt and a blazer that signifies success. Even though there are many people who have achieved great financial and business success who go to work in jeans and gym shoes, that was not my style.

Think about it for a moment. Most of those images and individuals that come to mind are in the business of selling their style(s) to consumers. What about the people who are paying them? How do they dress? What do they represent? Trend-seeking is exhausting and sometimes never-ending.

Who do you check in with to make sure that you have the right mix of clothes and shoes in your closet? Be careful of pursuing external validation. It places you in the mode of a vulnerable followership. In hindsight, God was propelling me to look and dress differently for preparation for the path and journey ahead. I couldn't afford to wear suits to school every day, and of course it would've been quite impractical.

My mother was a high-end resale shop connoisseur. She knew where the rich donated and even what times of the year. As we frequented the second-hand store venues, I was amazed at the price of 100% cotton shirts and tweed jackets. Shirts in excellent condition ranged from $1.25 to $2.50 and blazers were often under $5.00.

I had no idea that you could get so sharp and ready for the future inexpensively. I racked up on clothing, or to use one of the urban colloquialisms of that era, "I got geared up…" There was no more pressure to keep up or even act as though I cared what the latest trend was.

Do not conform any longer to the pattern of this world, but be transformed by the renewing of your mind. Then you will be able to test and approve what God's will is—his good, pleasing and perfect will.

— Romans 12:2

This was the new me. I was sharp with a 4.0 and a strong sense of confidence. However, I still needed a *plan*. Graduation was quickly approaching. One of my best friends in high school was a kid named Charo. He and I are still great friends to this day. In fact, we refer to each other as brothers. He was the first to notice my changes, and he began to study and hit the books just as hard.

Friends are very important. As you consider your friends and the influences that they have on you, are they good or bad influences? How do you influence others? The age-old cliché of birds of a feather flock together still holds true.

I wish to expound on that. Either you will become more like your crowd or your crowd will become more like you. Did I influence some of my closest friends to wear slacks and blazers to school? No, but I do believe that many of them began thinking with greater forms of individualism. I was starting to feel like an engineer in the making and understood that my environment and habitat for success were pivotal.

We moved on from hope and we're in the planning mode now. Can you envision what you want to do next? If so, start thinking, looking, planning, and preparing yourself to be what you desire to be. Also, assess how your current environment serves as an inhibitor or as catalyst to the fulfillment of your goals. I had to make some changes. First of all, I really couldn't hang out on the block because there was too much strife between various groups. But I had to get fresh air and liked being outside. I had friends from church and middle school that lived a few blocks over.

One Saturday afternoon, I was leaving out to visit a buddy a few blocks over and was confronted by the kid next door. He and I were the exact same age and were really good playmates in elementary school.

I used to go next door all the time and help him with his homework and try to encourage him to keep trying. "Why are you always gone and don't never kick it with us," he asked. "It is all good, I'm just busy most of the time," I responded. He emphatically inquired, "Oh, I know you don't think you better than nobody because you go to King and got all As?"

I guessed it was an accusation or, on second thought, perhaps it was a question. I don't remember having any discussion with him about how I was doing in school. Our mothers talked all the time, so that answers the question of how he knew how I was doing in school. "I'm just doing my thing, and handling my business," I replied while giving him dap and continuing to walk down the block.

That wasn't the last negative encounter with him. As the years progressed, the gap between our paths and outcomes continued to widen. Don't try to please your peers by being less than what God has for you to be. You will not have haters until you start doing well. Don't let them stop you!

> *If you belonged to the world, it would love you as its own. As it is,*
> *you do not belong to the world, but I have chosen you out of the world.*
> *That is why the world hates you.*
>
> *−* John 15:19

Examine your world and the world around you, circles of friends and personal space, starting at home. My home environment was very relaxed, for the most part. I had my own room at this point. Our home was a two-story, three-bedroom bungalow. One of the bedrooms served as the dining room and my mother's dressing room. My room was the up-stairs/finished attic portion of our home.

In my newfound success, I began to take notice of my new need for neatness and cleanliness. Everything didn't have to be meticulously clean, but I did reduce clutter in my room and tried to make sure that things remained in their rightful place. Order was a necessity considering my course loads and commute times.

I anticipated what a college dorm room would be like in comparison to my bedroom. What would a college campus community consist of?

Will there be any convenience stores, laundromats, and restaurants? These questions filled my mind, because I wanted to ensure fit. I wanted to fit into the new environment and to excel. I knew that I wanted to be an engineer for a long time. When I worked at the shop with my dad, I was fascinated by cars. He would remind me that I should consider trying to make them, as opposed to working on them. Making them, from his perspective, did not consist of factory work, but more so of being a design engineer. His only brother, James, who happened to be my favorite uncle, had just retired from working at Ford for 30 years. Us, Moorer men, were akin to hard work and sweat equity. However, they both wanted me to take a different route.

Faith and the great promise of the industrialized automotive industries in Michigan and Ohio brought them to the north from rural Alabama in the 1940s and 1950s. My mother was also born in the rural south (Nitta Yuma, Mississippi, to be exact). Her parents moved to Dayton, OH in the 1940s also. My parents met in Dayton, OH in the early 70s, fell in love, and married in 1973. As my father always said, the rest was history. Now, I found myself as a 17-year old with an understanding of my parents' past and their hopes for me. But without a clear picture of what my future would be like. I knew that I needed a *plan*.

Most of my friends wanted to stay local. Many of them had Michigan State University in mind as the college of choice. It was public, less expensive, close to home, great sports teams, good academic programs, and 'big-on-parties'. College fairs were a popular thing to do during Spring Break of junior year for all the kids who were either curious or truly wanted to go out of state. I wanted to stay close to home, partly because of my parents' age and health, and I really felt that Michigan had a lot of great colleges and universities.

By senior year, I was bombarded with college brochures, literature, and scholarship offerings. I was offered a full four-year academic scholarship to attend Michigan Tech University (MTU) in Houghton, MI. Houghton is about 500 miles north of Detroit. MTU had a solid engineering program, and it would've been free for me to attend except for books and meals.

I was pretty firmly set on MTU, until some admissions reps from GMI Engineering and Management Institute came to visit. "Students from our programs graduate in five years with a business/engineering degree and two and ½ years of corporate experience often from a Fortune 500 corporation..." exclaimed one of the reps. I eagerly asked, "So, I can get paid while I'm in school and get the degree?" She patiently responded, "Yes, and we have a dedicated corporate-relations staff that will work to get you placed at GM, Ford, or any other company that you desire."

I began to think ahead five years while assuming that I would have an edge on graduates from other schools because of my corporate experience. However, there were two major obstacles. The cost of the five-year program was slated as $75,000 and my ACT score was way too low. My composite ACT score was 19. I had hoped and planned for an opportunity like this. It seemed so close but yet so far. God will not tease you. He will show you your heart's desire, and he will also provide you the means to fulfill your dreams.

> *May he give you the desire of your heart and make all your plans succeed.*
>
> – Psalm 20:4

Many families face the challenge each year of trying to finance their children's education. We were no different. Financial aid, need-based scholarships, work-study, and income earned from the internships were said to be the resources that many students used to finance their education. I also needed to retake the ACT exam in order to get at least a 23 composite score to get accepted.

My high school's library had a lot of ACT prep books on reserve. I studied the prep books tirelessly for three weeks and did all the drills that I could possibly do. December 21, 1993, the day of the retest at GMI, had finally come. I asked my best friend Reggie to ride with me to take the test. In the discussion of having friends that have your back, or in colloquial terms, *"that are down for you"*, be sure that they are supportive of your positive ambitions. Likewise, be sure to be that type of friend to and for others.

The test started at 8:00AM. We left home at 6:00AM for an hour-long drive just to be sure to be there on time. Campus Center room 300 could seat 100 students, but there were about 20 test-takers that day. "God help me to do my best," I prayed. I took the test and drove back home to await the results. My ride was filled with anxiety, hope, and anticipation. Reggie felt my tension and asked, "How you think you did?" "Good, I think, or at least I hope," I said.

We got back to Detroit by midafternoon. Reggie went to the barber college to pick up some evening hours, and I went home to wait by the phone. At about 4:00PM, I got a call from the admissions rep. *"Hello, Is Cleamon Moorer available?"* I knew who it was, but my favorite response to callers that asked for 'Cleamon Moorer', are your looking for Jr. or Sr.? Her response was Jr., "I would like to inform you of our admission decision based upon your new ACT score. Your composite score is 28, and we would like to offer you admission at this time."

What was an obstacle a day ago was no longer a concern. The next mode of action was to work on the financial aid and complete the application file. We applied for every form of student-aid possible. Mrs. Burke, my high school guidance counselor, worked with me to get my resume in good shape in order to send it to my corporate relations manager at GMI.

Every high school student should have a resume. The resume should indicate a commitment to volunteerism, honor society membership, service-trips, part-time jobs, and a brief synopsis of academic performance and plans.

1994

During my last semester at King, my corporate relations officer worked diligently to place me with a company in the Detroit-metro area. I had the opportunity to phone and physically interview with three companies during a one-month period: GM Truck & Bus, Peterbilt, and ASC. I anticipated the GM interviews the most. The phone interview went very well. For the physical job interview, I had to drive to Troy, which is about 20 minutes north of Detroit. From time to time, it is imperative to get out of your comfort zone to receive what GOD has for you.

I drove to the GM management center anxiously and excitedly. To my surprise, it was a group interview, and several other incoming GMI freshmen were competing for positions. The facilitator of the interview presented a slide-show that detailed what to expect and what is to be expected of a GMI intern/ employee. She covered a complete assessment from start to finish, explaining how our college years could potentially catapult us into entry-level management in engineering capacities upon graduation.

Following the two-hour presentation, there was a Q&A forum used to get a feel of each candidate. In hindsight, I believe that this was sort of a process of elimination. Joy, excitement, and anxiety filled my heart and mind. I remember thinking, *"This is it; I will be going to GMI and training to be an engineer at the age of 18."*

As I drove home, I took note of all the visible differences between Oakland County's neighborhoods and my neighborhood. Why are there such obvious inequities in neighboring communities? Then some of my thoughts shifted to my journey so far. 20-25 minutes north of Detroit was much more affluent than where I was from. I went home feeling good and felt as if I got the job because I had been praying for it for quite a while. Am I a "sell-out," for trying to go places that I've never been before? Are making big plans and going for major goals a bad thing? Which company does God want me at? I hoped it was GM, because that is truly where I wanted to be.

Many are the plans in a man's heart, but it is the LORD's purpose that prevails.

– Proverbs 19:21

I knew that I had to call my friends and tell them how my interview went. It was all happening so fast. But God must have brought me this way, because MTU and its full-ride academic scholarship was what I initially thought was the path. Caught in the moment of realizing that I was a high school senior on the way to GMI and GM, it felt surreal. Soon as I walked in the door my mother asked, "Did you get it; how did everything go?" I tried to tell her everything about the drive to Troy, the interview, and the timetable ahead. Dad was coming in from work while we were still discussing the day's events.

He chimed in without any prior information of what transpired by saying, "You got it! I don't have any doubts about it. But you ain't seen nothing yet... keep walking with the Lord... you'll see." I wondered, "...how does he know this?" I haven't seen anything yet... what could be better than this? My father always made me think about how and why the Lord told him things that soon come to pass? "Would God ever talk to me like this?"

Understanding God and trying to hear the voice of the Lord was something that I never tried as a young kid or teenager, for that matter. God and I had sort of a "Santa Claus"- type of relationship. I considered how the ministers often preached that He was always watching, and we should ask Him for anything that we want. In the process of selective retention, the discussion pertaining to the commandments, long-suffering, repentance, and obedience never really stuck the way that the perks of Christianity resonated. Getting back to the perks, the letter of the official offer and the follow-up call came within a week of the GM interview.

Of course I accepted it. Senior Prom and HS graduation went by as a blur because I was focused on the exciting days ahead. Unlike for most high school graduates, there was no summer break. Classes at GMI started in July, and I had to be ready. However, I would be able to come back in October to begin three months of work at GM. My plan was set!

Now it was time to put it into motion. Go to GMI; work at GM for 5 years; graduate with an engineering degree; be a great engineer; and someday even become the CEO of GM. I also assessed my potential to be able to buy a house some day and have a beautiful wife and children.

The plan required having great fortune, being successful at every level, or did it? I could not conceive anything but success, because I had such a good plan, and I was on the track that God set me on. Right?

What about your plans? Will success derive solely from planning and working hard? Who plans for adversity and turmoil in their path to success? Could those ingredients yield greater success? As for me, I had no expectation of trouble; I only had the undeniable thirst and quest for success. Then was the time like no other to pursue it.

Chapter 3 – Pursuit of Success

Be strong and very courageous. Be careful to obey all the law my servant Moses gave you; do not turn from it to the right or to the left, that you may be successful wherever you go.

— Joshua 1:7

I thought that the night before leaving for college would be the ultimate evening to 'hang out'. Reggie and I had big plans, consisting of a highly anticipated and long-awaited double-date. However, it seemed as though my father had bigger plans. I will never forget this as long as I live; in fact, it probably was one of his best interventions up to that point.

I said, "Okay, Momma, I'll see you later," as I headed to the door. She calmly responded, "Your father wants to talk to you first." So, I did my usual knock on the door and stand in the doorway of their bedroom routine, "Yes sir Daddy?" He was wrapping up supper and to my knowledge, he hadn't been briefed on my plans for the evening.

"So what's this about, you headed out, you think?" He was gifted in that way, to ask you multiple questions at the same time while causing you to revisit the entire foundation of your proposal and campaign. "Yes sir, me and Reggie are just gonna kick-it for a little while," I replied. "Well, your mother tells me you have a big test tomorrow that helps to determine your future." I knew that he was talking about the math placement exam. He might've also known that I was going to try my best to make up for not having a summer vacation all in one evening. I confidently responded, "I'm ready for that test!"

He took his time to respond, "Even if you are, you still need a good night's rest. So forget about it!" That wasn't quite the end of the discussion as you probably can imagine. I was shocked and a little stunned, and perhaps it showed on my face; which is considered disrespectful by a lot of parents' standards. He continued with a greater justification of his position...

"You are not going to mess up if I can do anything to stop it... But if you go out tonight, and mess up in any kind of way at that school, don't look back here for any help or support for anything. Because you don't have your head screwed on right, you are putting the cart in front of the horse. You got plenty of time to run the street and chase girls. Now go on upstairs and get some rest..."

Talking about feeling dejected... my feet felt as though they were in quicksand. He didn't say that I can't go; he just laid the law on the consequences of failure. I was slow to move from the doorway. So, Dad got up from where he was sitting all 6 ft. 3 inches of him and began to approach me saying, "Now who are you looking at like that?" Of course, I quickly turned and walked away.

> *A wise son heeds his father's instruction, but a mocker does not listen to rebuke.*
>
> — Proverbs 13:1

The mental and physical diversion of a cold shower became a reality that evening, as I pondered over what the next day would bring.

Our drive up to Flint the next morning subdued all the hostility of the previous evening. Introspectively, I didn't once think about how they might be feeling or thinking about the days to come. I was stuck in my own whirlwind of anticipation. As we approached the campus and winded through the neighboring communities, I realized that this would be my new home for the next five years, right in the heart of Flint, MI. Remnants of the automotive industry were still alive and well. The town was a testament to a true blue-collar hard working racially diverse community at its finest.

The campus was comprised of three buildings. The dormitory, campus center (CC), and academic building were all connected through an underground tunnel. We retrieved my dorm-room assignment information in the grand lobby of the CC; and then we headed over to the dorm. My parents prayed and dad gave sort of a 'clear the air' type of speech, as we reconciled. What was so temporal seemed so final.

After 17 ½ years of togetherness the time had finally come for them to leave me. In all my packing, preparation, and pursuit of success, I never once considered how that moment would make me feel. Because now it was solely on me to make it happen. The "it", I defined as my pursuit of success. This pursuit, positive or negative, would define my substance. My hopes and planning phases up to that point were all based on prayer and faith. However, the work and the journey ahead was my sole responsibility. My parents did their part. Can I do this? Will it happen for me? Who is going to help me?

All these blessings will come upon you and accompany you if you obey the LORD your God:

– Deuteronomy 28:2

Beloved, I encourage you to keep making those steps toward pursuing success. You may feel alone at this juncture or at the crossroads ahead, but be sure to trust and obey God as you embrace the uncertain paths and journeys in your life.

I soon found that I wasn't alone. My dorm mate's parents were dropping him off as I escorted my parents out of the building. The dorm rooms were private, for the most part. We shared a phone in the middle of the wall and there was a sliding door that separated both rooms. The folks responsible for the move-in weekend had some ice-breaker events planned for the incoming freshmen following the placement exam. That very same night, I walked around the dorm unit and made acquaintances with a lot of the guys. Several of them were from Detroit and other Midwest cities and states.

The move-in committee also planned an off-campus ice-breaker which enabled all the guys in our unit to bond. I remember thinking that this is much more fun than I thought, but what is the catch? I knew that I had 18 credit hours (six classes) and that classes began the next day. My very first load consisted of Fortran 77, organic chemistry & lab, engineering graphics, pre-calculus, written & oral communication, and student orientation. I compared my schedule to other guys' schedules and realized that my course-load was the norm.

Another great benefit of socialization is taking the opportunity to learn and ask questions. There were a few sophomores in our unit that took the time to look over our schedules and give helpful critiques of each of our professors. Many of GMI's upperclassmen seemed glad to share information, insights, and even some of their old exams and quizzes.

Success is never achieved alone. In your pursuit of success, it is imperative to build alliances, networks, and bonds. Even in high school, it is pertinent to consider the people around you. Good friends and colleagues find ways to assist each other in achieving success.

The office of minority student affairs offered math and science-based weekly workshops and study sessions. Professors facilitated the sessions and opened them to all students.

During the first week of classes, the administration invited all of the new freshmen to a special meeting. The VP of Academic Affairs made a bold proclamation followed by a gentle request. "Look around you, to your right and left, in front of you and behind you. Three out of the five people around you will not be in here in five years. Some will transfer; some may drop out; and some will flunk out. However, only two out of five of you will graduate from GMI..."

I felt emptiness at the bottom of my stomach as his speech progressed. These were some very grim statistics. A 60% chance of not graduating resonated much louder to me than the 40% chance of graduating. His bold proclamation, coupled with my exhaustion, six courses, and work-study all began to take its toll on me.

All students were required to complete nine semesters in order to graduate. Senior year was comprised of three semesters to satisfy the thesis requirement. I looked ahead into the seemingly dismal future and assessed that I hadn't even begun to scratch the surface.

"Homesickness," doesn't quite describe what I felt. The "take it one-day-at-a-time" approach seemed as though it would take forever. I missed everything and everybody back home. Crying wasn't in my plan, but I was suddenly subdued by the big challenge ahead. Frequent telephone calls home and occasional letters from friends and family helped the time to go by. Furthermore, the reality of not wanting to turn back also fortified me.

I buckled down, went to study sessions, visited my professors during office hours, and studied with other students in the dorm. I made the adjustments of being on my own. My work-study job in the financial aid office, a meal plan, and a calling card met most of my physiological and psychological needs. I made a good friend by the name of Thomas earlier on in the term.

We often played basketball in the late hours of the evening following hours of studying. He had a thing for trying to act like Mike Jordan on the court, which wasn't unusual. It was the satire but not the substance of his game that is most memorable. B-ball and joking around was therapeutic. By the end of the term, classes had gone very well. I finished with a pretty high GPA, except for withdrawing from engineering graphics. The opportunity to go back home and start working at GM was the next exciting stop on the frontier.

I was assigned to the materials engineering department of GM's North American Truck Platform in Troy. This unit specialized in door panels, instrument panels, dashboards, seats, and carpet. For twelve weeks I learned from other engineers about how plastics are tested for tensile strength, utility, and dexterity. My weekly assignments were challenging. The assignment presented a steep learning curve. However, the adventure was exciting. My manager paired me with a different engineer each week to serve as their under-study and assistant. I loved what was coming out of my experiences.

Knowledge, pay, exposure, networking, and adventure were big perks. The biggest perk was occasionally having the opportunity to drive a car home each week. At 18, I truly believed I was pursuing success and the best was yet to come. Weekends as an intern were nothing like the weekends I spent during my senior year of high school. My academic performance had earned me a lot of freedom from my parents to do whatever I wanted to. I didn't have a curfew, but there was the concept of a decent and respectful hour.

Girlfriends; running the streets with Reggie; playing B-ball; and arriving late to church on Sunday mornings became my mode of operation. Should success disqualify you or make you exempt from living a wholesome God-fearing life? Alternatively, should we seek God more due to the great favor that he bestowed upon us to realize success? However, when it's about you and not about God, please be careful and do proceed with caution.

Only if life was all about driving nice cars at the expense of others and by the opportunities afforded by others, would there be any worries? Pragmatism was my governing doctrine. "This must be what God meant about abundance," I recall thinking.

The thief comes only to steal and kill and destroy; I have come that they may have life, and have it to the full.

— John 10:10

In your happiest moments do you think that God only wants you to be happy? Is your well doing an opportunity to help others and do more for

God? Are there any upcoming crosses to bear? How about valleys to cross? In the immaturity of self-centric thinking and the premature assessment of the path set before me, I thought it was all about me. When people are visibly doing well, some of us often use the colloquialism, "They are just doing their thing, or better yet, I'm just doing my thing." However, when things aren't going so well, are we still just doing our thing?

I returned back to GMI for semester two. A new load of courses and a retake of engineering graphics awaited me. Academically, things weren't going and didn't go as well as the first semester. I picked up another 18 credit hours comprised of Calculus, Principles of Chemistry & Lab, Engineering Graphics, Current Issues, and Economic Principles.

My study habits were the same as in the previous semester. The material was simply more difficult in each class. I finished the term by completing only 12 of the 18 credit hours that I attempted. I withdrew from my chemistry class in hopes of getting a different professor the following semester. I failed engineering graphics. My term GPA was somewhere in the C- range. The "F" in engineering graphics placed me on academic probation. Failure had become a reality. However, it was only an "F" in engineering graphics. Keyword 'engineering'... *if you can't pass engineering graphics, then how will you ever become an engineer?* This question haunted me.

The tongue has the power of life and death, and those who love it will eat its fruit.

— Proverbs 18:21

Self-doubt, pity, and decreased confidence had become my new mantle. What a difference six months made on my academic pursuits. I returned to GM for a new rotation. I was mentally marred by the looming academic probation status, but I tried to shake it off to embrace the plant engineering assignment. GM's academic coordinator of GMI students contacted me to discuss the seriousness of my academic probation status. She called to forewarn me about the academic success contingency for continued employment. "As long as you can remain in good academic standing with GMI, we got a place for you"…she reiterated at the close of our conversation.

To my surprise, I was assigned to mechanize all the plant's drawings that illustrated plant equipment, conveyors, manufacturing systems, and facilities into automatic computer aided drafting (ACAD). Even though I had failed mechanical drafting (engineering graphics), ACAD was a cinch. The mechanized drawings would be used to help engineers and planners assess opportunities to increase overall plant efficiency.

I met with vendors to plan plant upgrades and facility modifications. These meetings were a normal part of my weekly routine. Good performance evaluations from my managers and a 'see-saw' academic year defined my initial try at pursuing success. Year one had gone by all too fast. I was now a sophomore with six months of corporate experience. But I'd failed one course and I was on academic probation. I was carrying the burden of trying to live up to others' high expectations of me, coupled with a hefty load of self-doubt and discouragement. Do those components sound like they should be in the travel bags of someone pursuing success?

Come to me, all you who are weary and burdened, and I will give you rest.

– Matthew 11:28

Chapter 4 – Adversity Strikes

Although the Lord gives you the bread of adversity and the water of affliction, your teachers will be hidden no more; with your own eyes you will see them.

— Isaiah 30:20

1995

I found it difficult to holistically assess what I learned from year one. I gave it a good try, perhaps the best try yet in all of my years of academic pursuits. The time had come to return to campus for year two. I think I did a sufficient job of explaining my academic standing.

Academic probation should not be confused with academic warning. If grades do not improve in the subsequent semester, then more drastic measures are taken. I'd earned 27 of the 36 credit hours attempted. So in economic terms, I was charged for three courses that didn't result in a passing grade (two course withdrawals + one F). In addition, I was charged for a pre-calculus class during my first term. A pre-calculus course does not count as credits earned in most institutions. As you can tell, I definitely wasn't in position to apply for merit-based scholarships to help balance the deficit.

I decided to move off campus in an attempt to save money. Thomas and I ended up leasing a two-bedroom apartment a few blocks away from campus. This particular tenement wasn't ideal when you think of off-campus housing. It was quaint, muggy, and quite aged. Consider some of the budget urban hotels that double-up as apartments for guests.

We were living a ½ step above those standards without the tainted swimming pool and free HBO. It was okay, because the goal was to save money.

A whole new group of first-year students was arriving on campus. And, to my surprise, some of the students with "A-P standings" from prestigious high schools were coming in as first-year students with more credits earned than I had as a second-year student. So, I was a second-year student with freshmen classification. Was it embarrassing? Yes, it was embarrassing. The very same placement test from a year ago that landed me in pre-calc, landed some of them into Calculus II. Humility and a bit of eagerness to improve drove me.

My schedule consisted of Behavioral Science; Calculus II; Manufacturing Processes; Physics I; Principles of Chemistry; and Human Values in Art & Lit. I knew that I was in way too deep. However, this was the required course-load. I did most of my studying at our apartment and at the school's library.

The office of minority student affairs was very helpful. The office continued to offer workshops, seminars, and one-on-one tutoring sessions. As I peruse through my memory, I am taken back to week two of this term. Calculus II was a big challenge, coupled with Chemistry and Physics. In hindsight, I believe it was the combination of courses that caused the most trouble. I remember looking at my course-load as a set of two, three headed monsters.

I struggled on quizzes, homework, and labs in the science courses. Imagine the week of midterms. I was slipping fast and reaching to anything and almost anyone for assistance. The feeling of shame consumed me. In fact, it was often a joke and past-time to discuss and criticize people who were struggling.

Some of my new friends from Chicago brought the term "rocked" to our growing set of colloquialisms, if you failed a test. The term "banged" was also loosely used to describe the poor outcome(s) of assessments. If you did well, of course you "banged" it. Quite naturally, if you performed poorly, it "rocked" or "banged" you. My academic state of affairs was both "rocky" and all "banged" up.

It seems that this goes back to the whole locus of control discussion. When things are going well, it is human nature to take credit. This type of internal locus of control is accommodative to one's ego and need for self-importance. When things are going terrible, many of us turn to the notion of external locus of control. It is someone else's fault. But where was God in all of this? I started praying like never before in the heap of failing quiz after quiz.

If you falter in times of trouble, how small is your strength!

– Proverbs 24:10

Like many of us, I thought I could fix my own problems. My failures were rationalized and self-validated as the result of a number of factors. Some of the racial and social inequities started to bother me more than ever before. For instance, why was the pre-calc class predominantly made up of racial/ethnic minority students?

Even though the college was a predominantly white institution, there were some minority students who were performing very well. Many faculty members credited that to their high school preparation. I found myself at a point of trying to find any and every reason to explain or justify my poor performance.

Some of my thoughts pertaining to racism and bigotry were crystallized. Prof B was the head of the physics department. He was also my physics professor. One afternoon following a physics tutoring workshop, he brought a rather interesting discussion to me. "Cleamon, I have a new color copier in my office," he exclaimed. "*Okay*", why he is telling me this, I asked myself? "It can duplicate anything "colored" or of color, why don't you give me your photo ID and let's just see how well the resolution comes out." I replied, *"Maybe some other time."*

That was in the 90s and I was at a college an hour north of Detroit. It wasn't typical at all to hear these kinds of remarks on campus, especially from professors. An engineer from one of my previous rotations at one of GM's truck plants had offered a similar racially inappropriate discussion. During the first week, my engineering mentor provided an interesting play on words. "Okay Cleamon, what should I call you," he asked. I said, "Cleamon, Clem or Cle is just fine." He pondered for a brief moment and responded by saying, "I'll call you Clay, because your skin reminds me of what flower pots are made of; you know clay, mud, dirt?"

However, I never lashed out at neither one of those gentlemen. I knew that I needed them to help me to become an engineer. God knew that I was going to be black before he made me, right? I briefly thought, "…maybe I shouldn't have been pursuing engineering," because I was experiencing so much adversity.

> *Consider it pure joy, my brothers, whenever you face trials of many kinds, because you know that the testing of your faith develops perseverance. Perseverance must finish its work so that you may be mature and complete, not lacking anything.*
>
> – James 1:2-4

I felt like I didn't have some of the things that could turn my situation around. I focused on all of the things that I didn't have instead of on the things that I did have. It seemed as if money, privilege, a better academic preparation, and fraternal affiliation would solve my woes. Are you looking for things that you don't have in the midst of trials and tribulations to solve your problems? Can you recall thinking well only if I had… or only if I could? When you begin pulling and searching for things that you don't have, remember that you have God. He is, and He owns everything.

> *Let us fix our eyes on Jesus, the author and perfecter of our faith, who for the joy set before him endured the cross, scorning its shame, and sat down at the right hand of the throne of God.*
>
> – Hebrews 12:2

I owed the university a great deal of money that semester. I didn't have it. Private schools are generally more expensive than community colleges and public universities. My financial aid package simply wasn't enough to cover my expenses. I used my co-op earnings to pay the previous term's tuition.

My dad's business was not doing that good at the time. The reality of his age began to hit me, coupled with my mother's health issues. She did not have a terminal disease, but she was plagued by several immune system deficiencies.

In addition, my dad's only brother's health was in dire straits. Uncle James was the coolest. He wanted me to pursue engineering and to do well. He and his wife, Aunt Mary, would often visit us growing up. My father wasn't big on entertaining guests, for that matter. When it came to visiting, we frequently went out of town to see relatives, for the most part.

So, I knew that he really cared for his brother in the deepest meaning of the term. He was also very successful. Uncle James owned several apartment buildings in Detroit. He lived in a beautiful home. Uncle James was an ordained deacon. He and Aunt Mary were the model couple in my eyes. All of their children were grown and doing well. Needless to say, he was certainly my favorite uncle.

Uncle James also had a new Cadillac Fleetwood Brougham, which he often let me borrow or chauffeur for him around town from time to time. However, there is a season for everything. I wasn't prepared for his season of sickness and disease, but it was evident that his health was declining.

I didn't want to add to my parents' issues by making constant phone calls home explaining my circumstances and predicament. I reminded myself that they did their part when they raised me and brought me up in a Christian home.

One of the most daunting factors of failure is the loss of control. Consider walking on ice or sleet. Do you ever recall the pre-fall? In the pre-fall, some of your muscles tense up in an attempt to avoid the fall. It seems that they "tense up" and fear of the fall or slippage is equally if not more painful than the fall itself. However, the fear of the fall sometimes overtakes the moment.

My fear of being a flunkout began to embody the fabric of my thoughts and actions. By final exams' week, I was tired and bushed. Thomas and I decided to go on a 72-hour study binge.

We stayed at the apartment studying from Friday afternoon to the wee-hours of Monday morning. I had the worst feeling going into finals. It was so much information to remember. However, exam performance is not all about memorization. Having the ability to perform and build on conceptual understanding when prompted or solicited, is the key. I needed God to help me. This was the first time that I had ever prayed with such great desperation. I prayed until I was speechless.

With every fiber of my physical and moral being I shouted, *"Dear God, please make me an engineer!"* I didn't know how he would do it. But I knew he could because it was apparent that I couldn't do it. I cried on the floor and on my pillow for several minutes. I knew that if God didn't step in soon, I was going to flunk out of college. The next day, I walked down the street to the academic building with great fear, anxiety, and loaded with caffeine.

Taking six exams in four days was not the issue. I drew blanks, performed incompetently, and battled stress, for all four testing days. I was glad when the end of the week came, because it was time to move out and go back to work. If I actually did as bad as I thought I did, then going to work at GM would be very temporary.

My third work-term was very exciting. I was placed at Milford Proving Grounds in the test engineering department. I benchmarked competitors' materials, dashboard components, and instrument panels in comparison and contrast to our current SUV lines. This was a great time for me in comparison to the prior semester. I was back at home and I could see how my parents were doing first-hand.

I visited Uncle James several times while he was in the hospital. However, I couldn't bring myself to tell him about what I was going through. We talked more about him getting well, sports, and cars. How long would it take for my secret to be revealed? Revealing my failures wouldn't only change how others viewed me, but I would have to accept that it didn't work out. Or, maybe I didn't work out.

Generally, it took two weeks for grades to come in the mail. When they finally came, I read my transcript and it made me feel like I swallowed a cantaloupe. It was one thing to perceive failure, but realizing it, is another thing. The grades read as follows:

Calculus II:	65 (F)
Physics I Mechanics:	65 (F)
Principles of Chemistry:	65 (F)
Human Values in Art and Lit:	65 (F)
Manufacturing Processes:	76 (D)
Behavioral Science:	70 (D)

Credits Earned: 7   Credits Attempted 23

This was my worst semester ever. Perhaps this might've been one of the lowest GPAs for all students in the history of the college. Oh if my path and journey stopped there, you might not have ever heard this story.

Reading the report card brought so much anguish back then. I can smile now when discussing this, because I see just how far God has brought me. However, the worst was yet to come. The department of academic affairs takes extreme measures against grades like these. They didn't take my failure lightly at all. I was not academically fit to continue my education at the college.

Consider a boxing match that has to be waived off by the referee and declared a technical knock-out (TKO) by judges. Sometimes the beaten and battered incumbent doesn't know why the fight is being stopped. He might not even know his name and definitely not his mother's maiden name at the time. However, he thinks that he wants to go on. I was there, I wanted to go on. I had no wherewithal to go forward.

The office of academic affairs did not make me wait long at all. I received their letter the following week.

Cleamon Moorer, Jr.

This letter is to inform you that your cumulative academic performance at GMI through this past Summer Term meets the criteria for "academic dismissal" as described on page 37 of the 1995/1996 GMI catalog. Therefore, your student status is scheduled to be terminated effective Friday...

It had happened. The letter did offer some recourse. It offered an opportunity to petition the academic dismissal decision. Alternatively, of course, non-petitioning would result in a confirmed academic dismissal. One of my biggest mistakes was not talking to anyone about this. I didn't make any attempt to reach out to anyone at the college to help me write the appeal letter. *"I can do the best job of explaining what went wrong."* I composed and submitted my appeal letter before the deadline.

Work served as a pleasant distraction. The test track at the proving grounds served as an outlet. I took Corvettes and Pontiac Ram-Airs out on the track several times a week. I hit the slopes and courses. Once again, I was clinging to materials and status. Many people grasp to things, people, and even substances to brace their fall or to nurse the wounds of the fall.

On a positive note, the 'Million Man March', led by Minister Louis Farrakhan, was a great diversion for me at the time. The historic march successfully brought men of color together to envision community building, personal development, and commitment to positive change. This peaceful demonstration was a monumental success. I was at work on the day of the march juggling my own personal woes. I was inspired and strengthened by the positive communication and dynamics taking place in many of my social circles.

Diversions often offer us a means to cope. However, be watchful of diversions that easily turn into vices. Marijuana, liquor, self-indulgence, and lust/covetous behaviors are temporary fixes that could potentially have long-term negative effects.

I didn't have an extreme taste for anything. This was a dangerous place to be mentally. This sense of mental and spiritual wandering left me open or vulnerable to self-pity and doubt. Self-pity can be just as damaging as any of the other aforementioned diversions.

Take my yoke upon you and learn from me, for I am gentle and humble in heart, and you will find rest for your souls. For my yoke is easy and my burden is light.

– Matthew 11: 29-30

The academic review committee moved quickly to make their decision. They made a unanimous decision to terminate my academic status effective immediately. The provost forewarned me that my corporate sponsor would be notified of this decision. My reasons and explanation detailed in my appeal letter were simply not good enough. However, the college gave me three options.

a. You can move forward with your life and we wish you all the best in your academic and professional pursuits.

b. You can enroll in another college/university for a year and retake all of your failed courses. Then reapply for admission into GMI next year.

c. You can reapply one year from now to be readmitted on a 'Student at Large' basis and on Academic Probation.

I was heartbroken and downtrodden. However, I can now offer you a remedy for facing great adversity. When adversity strikes, try to envision yourself in a four-room apartment. I learned this concept later in graduate school.

Contentment Upstairs (Room 1)	**Renewal** Upstairs (Room 2)
Denial Downstairs (Room 3)	**Anger** Downstairs (Room 4)

When facing adversity, change, and life in general, try to remain upstairs in room two. We have to always be in renewal mode. Strive for continuous improvement, modification, and renewal in all areas of your life. It is easy for me to share this with you now.

But at the time, I stayed in rooms three and four for a longer period of time than I needed to.

My boss called me into his office to give me my 1995 GMC Jimmy Development Team "Truck of the Year" certificate and polo shirt. I guess that he couldn't help but mention his knowledge of my academic status. *"This is sort of like a going away present for you, I understand."* His cynicism couldn't have been any more untimely. However, this was his way of telling me that I had a scheduled meeting with human resources and the GMI co-op coordinator.

The meeting was really an exit interview. I had to surrender my badge and ID/Access cards. My co-op coordinator was always polite and considerate.

She seemed baffled by my quick fall. With the deepest look of concern on her face she asked, "What happened?" I went into the same discussion that I shared with the academic review committee in my appeal letter. But the outcome was the same. "Well you had such great promise to become an engineer someday. If you ever get back in the good graces of GMI, feel free to give us a call. We will see if we have a place for you then." She said it all with compassion and a smile. However, it didn't lighten the reality of failure.

I was terribly dejected. I got fired from GM and kicked out of school. What happened to my plan? My pursuit of success had come to a screeching halt. All that was hoped for was gone too quickly. "I got to tell my friends that I'm not going to be on campus next semester." Even worse, my parents will know that I no longer work for GM, and I flunked out of engineering school. However, what about my prayer during final's week: *"Dear God, please make me an engineer!"*

I left the GM facility for what appeared to be the he last time, consumed by the illusion of despair and grounded by failure.

What is more, I consider everything a loss compared to the surpassing greatness of knowing Christ Jesus my Lord, for whose sake I have lost all things. I consider them rubbish, that I may gain Christ

– Philippians 3:8

Chapter 5 – Despair

1996

Cast all your anxiety on him because he cares for you.

— I Peter 5:7

My hopes of becoming an engineer had dissipated. I had thought that my plan was fool-proof. I always thought that when you do your very best, things just fall in line. The truth is that my best wasn't good enough. However, I prayed when I was in trouble. Did I somehow stop praying when things were going extremely well?

Well, I know that I wasn't fellowshipping at a local church near GMI. Other students weren't either, or were they? None of my close friends seemed to miss or mention church on Sunday mornings, except for Thomas. He would drive back to Detroit some Sunday mornings to play the keyboard for his church. However, he was getting paid to do that.

Somehow, I began to believe that going to church and praising God was independent of academic success. It became optional and then obsolete. I needed to fellowship in church, but I was struggling so much that I either decided to study, eat, or sleep in on Sunday mornings.

But seek first his kingdom and his righteousness, and all these things will be given to you as well.

— Matthew 6:33

If you are in a rut, you should seek God immediately. Don't hesitate or delay. Throw popular opinions out. In fact, it is imperative to pray without ceasing. Let's not seek God only when we are in trouble. And by all means don't fall into the norm of society and popular culture of being independent of God, or simply referring to Him as a "higher being."

Some people use the phrase: "*Oh God, I am going to need you for this one…*" We need him for everything that is worthwhile. Now getting back to the story, I wasn't aware of my continuous need for God's direction, guidance, mercy, and strength at that time.

I got home from my exodus from GM and spoke with my parents in great depth about the matter. My mother immediately assumed that I was victimized. In her opinion, it was a travesty and a shame that the school kicked me out and that GM followed suit. I love her for that and for so many other things. But I didn't want or need a gentle pat on the head nor the illusion that "they-all" plotted against me.

You reach a point where you have to be for real with yourself. I had blown it in a major way. No mother's compassion should ever blur the vision of reality and truth. All of her compassion wouldn't help me get past that juncture or put plans in motion to move forward. Compassion with a compass headed in the right direction is imperative.

However, old Dad, on the other hand, seemed to be primed for these types of pep talks and kicks in the rear. I don't know if it was due to his experience or a combination of wit and grit. My mother called him at the shop to alert him of the catastrophe. With all of her emotions, you would've thought that I had been decapitated by a mob of pagans.

He asked to speak to me, and I knew it was going to be an interesting conversation, to say the least. "So, you're finished, just like that huh?" The dichotomy of his query left me reeling for the right response. "Well, they say I can't come back for a year or so," I explained. He quickly followed by asking, "…and then what or now what?" I replied, "I guess I got to go to a community college and try to get back in, but I don't know about my job or engineering…" I said little, but for him, I had either said enough or too much.

He calmly but assertively cut in, "Life is hard, ain't nobody giving away anything. If you really want something worth having, you have to sacrifice for it. It may require bleeding, sweating, and even crying to get it. Just ask the Lord to help you out along the way. Take breaks, but don't break away from it. Everything is going to be alright if you don't break down like a little sissy every time things don't go your way. Are you still there?" I was trying to process all of this information and think of a crafty response to it. "Yes sir, I'm still here." He saluted with one of his most common requests, "…alright, let me talk back to your Momma."

I'm sure they dealt with the disappointment in their own way. Surprisingly, my father didn't seem disappointed. I don't know if he expected me to fail or expected that somehow I would overcome it. Enough of dealing with their thoughts, I had too many of my own to deal with.

How long must I wrestle with my thoughts and every day have sorrow in my heart? How long will my enemy triumph over me?

– Psalm 13:2

I wouldn't be driving company cars home for the weekend anymore. I'm back on the block. Talking about regression, but the bible uses the term pruning. What does it mean to be off for a year? I got a year to try to make up for all the errors and shortcomings of the previous year. Working was imperative; I needed some money and a confidence-builder. I had picked up a job at a shoe store in the mall, before I left GM. Amos had helped to get me a job in the shoe store business back in 1992. It was a natural fit to continue selling shoes while I was at GM to make some extra money.

So, the new plan consisted of enrolling into a community college and working at the shoe store. What a downgrade, hunh? I went from GMI to a community college and from GM to Florsheim shoes. How arrogant was it for me to look down and view the status of others so condescendingly? When God allows us to be reduced, we have to trust that it is for our own good.

For whoever exalts himself will be humbled, and whoever humbles himself will be exalted.

– Matthew 23:12

You see, I was placed on an inflated pedestal very early in life, from being a Parker Player all the way up to the National Honor's Society and Who's Who of American High School students. Somehow I either forgot the journey or didn't recognize who made all good things possible.

Merit and success are great to achieve. Success coupled with humility and integrity is even better. Now when you can combine your humility and integrity with your success, then you are on the ball. The pedestal deflated and on came the nylon foot socks and foot scale. Oh yes, measuring feet, stocking inventory, and scurrying to get the right size and choice for a customer, became the mode of operation. This was honorable and honest work. My income was just enough to help me pay my tuition.

I never knew how inexpensive community college could be. I enrolled into Oakland Community College (OCC) to re-take all the failed courses. OCC had some great instructors and students from all over the Detroit metropolitan area. Some students opted to study pre-engineering for the first two years and then transfer to a bigger school to complete a bachelor's program.

The setting was very diverse. Students of all ages and walks of life starting a career, changing careers, or returning for personal reasons filled the classrooms. For the first time in a long time, I didn't have any distractions.

I got back into the regimen of attending church each Sunday and actually listening to the sermons. I joined the men's choir. Thank God for knowing our hearts, because I truly am not a vocalist. But I wanted to praise and seek Him. It is amazing how we can worship and listen effectively when we really need to hear from the Lord. Our ears should fervently and attentively be in tune to what God is saying and doing all the time.

My professors were very approachable and my new classmates were cordial and enthused to be learning. Calc II and Physics made so much more sense the second time around. Calc II is meant to be taken once, but not twice. However, I found myself glad to be repeating these courses, because I wanted to master them.

Study groups and tutoring sessions still remained a part of my regimen. The difference of being at home and commuting to the campuses vs. living away was a huge benefit for me. I am a firm believer in the efficacy of community college programs. They are just the right option for many students, and they prepare them to charter the next academic or professional path.

I was making decent money at the shoe store from my sales commissions. But I still desired to be an engineer someday. Midterm exams had come and gone. I passed all of them with high marks. My schedule allowed me to help Dad out at the shop and to catch up on visiting family and friends.

One day I decided to go and check on Uncle James. He was home and seemed to have recovered from most of his ailments. We had an enjoyable time, laughing, and catching up on the current events.

He wanted me to move his truck and trailer from the backyard to the street. I couldn't figure out how to do it. The angle of the truck and the width of the driveway weren't working in my favor. My cousin, Mitch, lived in a house right next door to his Dad; so he decided to come over and give us a hand. Uncle James' last words to me were "*...don't make it so long, the next time you come to see me, you hear?*"

Had I known that was the last time I would see him alive, what would I've said or done differently? Was I so caught up in my struggle that I lost sight of the dilemmas of those closest to me? I caution that we can't afford to get overly consumed in our own trials and tribulations.

Do take the time to check on the elders, friends, and neighbors. God wants us to pray for others and be concerned with each other more than ourselves.

> *Be devoted to one another in brotherly love. Honor one another above yourselves.*
>
> — Romans 12:10

The year brought good and bad events, and it wasn't half-way over yet. I learned in time to take my uncle's ascension into Heaven as a good thing. To see the transformation of a saint and the toll it takes on survivors is sometimes indescribable.

My dad had other children from previous relationships. Out of my four siblings, Diane was by far my favorite. Diane came to Uncle James' funeral. She was a part of my life for as long as I can remember. Diane and my mother were only a few years apart in age. Thus, I have a niece and some nephews who are older than me. However, all of that is beside the point. She came to visit at a very pivotal time in my life.

It is more than imperative to create a habitat for success. Not just where you live, but also the people who are around you are just as essential. Be sure that your habitat is clean and conducive for success. Understanding and wisdom can help to safeguard and establish your habitat.

Diane stayed with us for a while after the funeral. We shared insights and compared our upbringings and experiences. She helped me to understand my father's evolution and his perspective on things. I only knew that he was wise and stern.

However, some of my father's paths and journeys were mysteries to me. Our dialogues encouraged me to reason with him to get a better understanding on direction and guidance. For most of my life, I only accepted what he said out of respect, reverence, and fear.

Now that I'd become a young man, it was time to explore and conceptualize my understanding of life into a broader framework. Eventually, he shared more with me pertaining to his troubled childhood and lack of parental guidance. I was fortunate to have most of his siblings and their children in the same city with us.

Please take the time to study your family's origin and sociology in the context of spirituality and advancement. You will find that the same God that brought mercy and many blessings to them years ago is still available to bless you today.

My mother's parents were also blessed people. Her father passed when she was 11. But I, similar to the songwriter, Helen Baylor, had a praying grandmother. Grandma Howard did not take any mess. She was a single mother who raised seven children in the heart of one of Dayton Ohio's housing projects.

Grandma was a proud and strong woman in every sense of the terms. We visited her and my aunts and uncles several times a year. I remember most how Grandma prayed. You could catch her singing, praying, and cooking as early as 5:00AM in the morning. She was a mother of the church and would break out into a "hymn" anytime during the service. Best of all, the congregation would follow suit as Mother Howard sang.

All of her children made time for us when we came to visit. They all grew up to be successful and did not stray from Grandma's teaching. I am so thankful for them and my host of cousins. In that, I realized that I had to succeed. It was no longer an option. We all came from God, the Father, and he made us to succeed and to be victorious.

> *So God created man in his own image, in the image of God he created him; male and female he created them.*
>
> — Genesis 1:27

I'm sure someone you know or know of has succeeded. Look for the best in everyone that you encounter. Start with your relatives, past and present. Examine the character, virtues, and moral fiber of people. In today's society, mass media and popular culture often times replaces the importance of integrity and discipline, with glamour and material wealth. I concluded that it was in me to succeed, because of who made me and the ones before me.

So, if all this was true, then why had I failed? The world of GMI was moving on without me. Students had completed the winter term of 1996 and were getting geared up for the summer term. I was out of the mix at GMI and off track. I didn't directly correspond with any of my former classmates.

I heard through the grapevine that someone noted that I'd dropped out. *"I think he's attending a community college, trying to gang-bang, and hoop a little bit."* It was totally absurd, because the gang-banging part was so far from the truth.

Some people will ride you down. There is always someone to run back and tell you indirectly what is being said about you. My word of advice is to pray for your fans and foes. Love them just the same. Sure, I was displaced and seemingly disadvantaged. However, just a year ago,

"I was where they are." It was not funny by any stretch of the imagination. Dealing with failure and renewal isn't an easy task. It can be lonesome and challenging.

Will I ever get back on track? That question haunted me when I was off track. I could only wonder what God was setting me up for. I refused to believe that He had brought me to that point to leave me or forsake me.

Whatever He was setting me up for had to be great. He took the time to set me aside to get my attention. Does God have your attention? Do you need a time-out or to be set apart to be set up? If you are off track, don't panic. This may very well be where God wants you right now!

> *"But sir," Gideon replied, "if the LORD is with us, why has all this happened to us? Where are all his wonders that our fathers told us about when they said, 'Did not the LORD bring us up out of Egypt?' But now the LORD has abandoned us and put us into the hand of Midian."*
>
> – Judges 6:13

Chapter 6 – Set-Up

Could this be where God wanted me to be? If so, then why didn't I just start there? Why did I have to be humiliated and lose so much in the process? I could have saved a whole lot of money if I'd started out at a community college in the first place. Did I fool myself from the very beginning? Anyhow, I was doing very well at OCC.

I began to look forward to going to class every other day. Socialization should get easier as we move forward. Every new encounter with different colleagues should become easier. I think that it was harder to socialize because of my crimson stain. Sometimes, some of us carry baggage, regret, and inner turmoil. This can affect our ability to interact with others. We're often concerned and even petrified that someone else will find us out for who we really are. So, some of us live a façade.

As a 19-year old, I felt that I had to stay true to my bravado. In this case, the issue was still not fully me or my shortcomings. It was a combination of circumstances and a change of the tide. And if I kept to myself, then I believed I could be myself. I thought that if I began to interact with some of my new peers, the discussion of my past failure would've come up. Who plans to fail? I was so tired of hearing clichés. *"If you fail to plan then you plan to fail!"* I still don't know which motivational speaker takes credit for this pearl of wisdom. I planned to soar but ended up sore.

And we know that in all things God works for the good of those who love him, who have been called according to his purpose.

— Romans 8:28

My course schedule consisted of Tuesday and Thursday classes, which gave me time to ponder all of these queries and quotes. I had the flexibility of taking more than just retakes. A course titled 'Organizational Behavior' (OB) caught my attention on the course schedule. My entire outlook on organizations, people, and even sociology began to change from the moment that I signed up for the course. The professor was an industrial psychologist, named Dr. Sobol.

The OB class met every Tuesday and Thursday from 1:00PM to 2:20PM. He used a textbook called, *'The Human Side of Organizations'*. The cover of the textbook featured a sprinter on a track in the take-off position. I didn't know the significance or irony of the metaphor then. The runner on the track signified competition and of course being in contention.

What track was I on at the time? I felt off track. In terms of contention, I was contending with failure. However, what number does the runner failure wear? Where is he on the track? Failure was behind me. I was in a position to sprint forward and catch up to a positive fate. I was thinking too deeply if it was solely based on the cover of a book.

Dr. Sobol's lectures were both interesting and humorous. He took complex topics and applied them easily to some of the current events across various industries. The chaotic nature of some companies and the lack of motivation of many of their employees puzzled me. From a systems-perspective, I began to realize that discord is acceptable.

Failure and success often work in tandem on an organizational level. Since groups of people work together to comprise an organization, then it must be prone to flaws. People are flawed, from the CEO all the way down to the disenchanted co-op student. However, each entity is needed at different times and positions in an organization to make it all work. I realized then and at that point that I loved 'OB'!

I left each lecture with a greater understanding than I gathered from reading the text the prior evening. I didn't recall seeing an OB course offering at GMI. Who knew that OB would end up playing such a pivotal role in my life? I was applying it to my experiences at C&M Collision, Florsheim Shoes, GMI, and GM. My struggle to make sense of machine bureaucracy and varying business models consumed the text of my written course assignments. How else would I have gotten to know OB and apply it to past, present, and future professional and business scenarios, if I had not been taken off track?

> For I know the plans I have for you," declares the LORD, "plans to prosper you and not to harm you, plans to give you hope and a future.
>
> – Jeremiah 29:11

If you are ever displaced or feel off track, try to find a passion. Do something different. Consider an abstract painting on a wall. A beautiful abstract painting can take the viewer on a metaphysical journey. One's sensory channels attempt to interpret the drawing. We search for meaning and resonance with our own perspectives, thoughts, and experiences. Often when there isn't any resonance, we are either intrigued, or we dismiss it. Try not to be quick to dismiss the things that don't immediately resonate with you. Consider pursuing more than what simply intrigues you.

I was so engaged in the pursuit of engineering that I dismissed anything that seemed the least bit abstract. God has given us both the arts and the sciences. They work in tandem. The world and its ecosystem are both beyond measurable beauty and the understanding of scientologists.

However, where did OB exist in the realm of all of this? It served as the glue for me. I started to see that even if I was to become an engineer, I would still first be an employee within an organization. My success as an engineer would be contingent upon the success of others and the system as a whole. I began to apply a systems-view in light of my recent failure.

Systems are comprised of inputs, processing, and outputs. I obviously omitted worship and praise as key inputs. My information processing and conceptual understanding was diluted. I was consumed by my financial-aid woes, my parents' well-being, fear of failure, and flawed self-perceptions. Those distractions rarely gave me a clear vision. And as for the outputs of that particular system design, need I say more?

Failure is often the result of a flawed system. Consider recalibrating the processing of your own system and its subsystems. I often went into final exams' week full of Mountain Dew and doughnuts. Caffeine and sugar give you a temporary boost of energy, but these ingredients don't sustain you. Giving too much care and concern about what people think and say about you can also cause system malfunction.

Praying and worrying about circumstances is another catalyst to system breakdown. When you pray and worry you put yourself in neutral on the up-side of a decline. Try to picture that. The negative forces and influences neutralize your positive energy. Don't ask God to help you with a problem, and then take it back from God to toil it for yourself. Whose problem is it? Our dilemmas are God's opportunity.

Getting back to my time at OCC, I was supposed to take the courses that I failed and stay solely fixated on the engineering curriculum. Taking OB didn't seem practical at the time. Be careful and watchful of practical or pragmatic thinking. "Practical" by origin stems back to the 13th century Old French translation of "being fit for action." Think about some of God's miraculous works and wonders. Does making a human being from the dust of the earth seem "fit for action," in our myopic scheme of things?

God isn't practical. He doesn't have to practice anything. Imagine God practicing to make the universe. How about rehearsing the *"Let There Be..."* commands? He does not have to abide by anyone's modern conventions nor by any of our expectations of logical explanations.

I will instruct you and teach you in the way you should go; I will counsel you and watch over you.

— Psalm 32:8

His brilliance is beyond words and our greatest imagination. But it doesn't prevent Him from communicating with us. It should also not stop us from seeking, hearing, and listening to and for the voice of God. It may start out faintly but the directions will become very distinctive over time. For me, OB simply started out as a hunch. However, I trusted that it was a step in the right direction and a means to get back on track.

After taking OB, I signed up to retake physics. I learned a lot about physics in high school, and I thought I was on track to do well in it in college. Physics was offered once a week at the furthest OCC campus from me. The commute was about 40 minutes one-way, but it was so worth it.

The professor was enthusiastic about teaching the course and explaining concepts. English wasn't his first language and from time to time students would ask him to repeat things. He was patient and sharp. It seemed that he enjoyed teaching from the overhead projector more so than the dry-erase board. This especially helped me to be able to watch as he set up problems, diagrams, and equations. Best of all, he allowed us some in-class break-out time to work with our peers on the homework assignments.

In one of the break-outs, I met a real cool guy, who became a good study partner throughout the term. For the sake of reference, let's call him Jake. Jake was about eight years older than me. This was also his second shot at college. We met on Saturday evenings at his apartment to study physics and to complete homework assignments. He was married, and the father of an adorable two-year-old daughter. I totally felt free to be myself around him. During one of our study sessions, I shared my recent bout with engineering and failure with him. He emphatically replied by saying, "...that isn't nothing, everybody got a story. Yours isn't as bad as mine."

His story sounded good, for the most part. Sure he was a little older than me. Community colleges are filled with students of all ages. He had a nice car, an apartment, and a beautiful family. Jake had plans to seek better employment upon completion of his associate's degree.

Initially, I didn't understand what could have possibly been so bad. "I flunked out too! I was going to school in Atlanta, and I started selling drugs while on campus.

I partied; I drank; and smoked weed almost every day. The "life" was much sweeter to me than going to school, but I'm paying for it now." I took in all that he said and I wanted to jump in with questions. I didn't ask a lot of questions because I wanted him to keep telling his story. I empathetically responded by saying, "But look at you now, it is all good now."

He went further to explain that he had mouths to feed and didn't want to end up in the penal system. In further conversations, we talked about how God blessed him with a family. "My family changed my life," he said. This type of scenario was not foreign to me. Some of my best friends from middle school and high school got caught up in the fast-life.

I wasn't "sheltered" from the streets and bad choices growing up. I decided early that I didn't want any part of it. My dad's shop was on Livernois Avenue. Livernois offered all the staples of street-life. Liquor stores, fast-food restaurants, adult-entertainment, barber & beauty salons, and automotive-related businesses aligned north and south.

Some of the shop's best paying customers were accused of making a living from the proceeds of the underworld. I'm sure that some of these same negative elements were also prevalent in Oakland County. Perhaps the same negative constructs were not as prevalent and definitely not focused on by the media to the same degree. I learned it doesn't matter where you go or where you are from. There are vices, traps, and pitfalls everywhere. What matters is *WHO* you take with you. Be sure to take God along with you from the low points and to the high points.

I remained focused on God and my classes at OCC. I still remained aware of what was happening in and with the streets, professional sports, the local economy, and popular culture. Balance became much easier to achieve. I found myself studying for each course every day. Regardless of homework assignments or quizzes, I studied additional hours anyway. I honed in on good college-level study habits.

Try to incorporate who you are into what you do regularly. By this I mean, don't disown being a Christian or a student in any of your various settings. While selling shoes, I kept in mind that I was still a student on the path to becoming an engineer.

Sometimes, some of us abort our identity to fit in with our present environments. You can be versatile and relate to anyone while remaining true to who you are. One of my managers, at the shoe store, often spoke badly about people pursuing higher education. He occasionally bragged, *"Look at me, I haven't gone to anybody's college, and I run this whole store!"* This was true. That may have been fine for him, and it may have met his family's needs sufficiently.

As for me, I wanted more. Thus, I would just nod my head and tell him that he was doing fine. It wasn't my place to argue with him and make him accept, appreciate, and understand my ambition and motivation. I mentioned this because in the flow of being who you are, you must be creative regardless of the environment.

I often decided to read and study in one of the bookstores or in the food court of the mall. Those locations were much more conducive to study than the backroom of the shoe store.

In this stretch of being off track, I learned to trust God. Only God can give you joy in the midst of trials and tribulations. He can turn your humiliation into humility. God has a way of restoring and redirecting your paths to get you on the track that He desires for you to be on. Attending OCC and working at the shoe store was different from what I set out for. But ultimately this redirection was better than the path that I was originally on. It wasn't humiliating, it was humbling.

> *Trust in the LORD with all your heart and lean not on your own understanding; in all your ways acknowledge him, and he will make your paths straight.*

> — Proverbs 3: 5-6

This path was fulfilling and rewarding. I was also able to spend a lot of time getting to know my father better. He was at the shop most of the time while I was growing up. The time that we spent together in the evenings when I was a child was very limited. Now that I was a young adult, things were a lot different. I gained some life experiences that helped to make our conversations more interactive.

My mother was periodically hospitalized for routine exams and procedures. So, Dad and I spent a lot of evenings together. He shared stories and testimonies from his life experiences that changed my life forever. After sharing a bucket of chicken, coleslaw, and a two-liter bottle of orange soda, we were set for heavy dialogue.

He was well versed in everything from world affairs to biblical scriptures and everything in between. He always talked about how life had been hard for him, but God always saw him through. I wanted to explore and go further now that I was experiencing the hand of God in my time of trial. So, on one of our evenings together at the house, I decided to probe. "Give me an example of how God delivered you when you didn't see any other way out."

He took his time to respond after meticulously wiping away the chicken crumbs from his face. "Well, God has helped me so many times, so let me think of a good one. Oh here is a good one, the time we were down to our very last. On a Thursday night, I gave your mother the last little bit of money that I had to my name. She went to the store and bought some dinner with it. I was worried out of my mind, because I did not know where the next meal was coming from. There were no cars in the shop, and I didn't have any customers. All of you all ate that night, but I just snacked on some of the food. I couldn't sleep. So I came out of the bedroom and sat down on the floor right here beside the couch. Then I decided to get on my knees and pray to God like I've never prayed before. I talked to God, just like I'm talking to you right now. And... I told him that I would not get up off of the floor until he answered me. I needed him to tell me what to do to feed my family. So after a while, the Spirit of God told me by 12 o'clock tomorrow afternoon you will have money to pay your bills and feed your family."

I was sitting on the edge of the couch, because I really wanted to know what actually happened the next day. He continued talking, "...now this is the truth. The next day I got up to go to the shop and wait on God to meet me there. 9:00AM, 10:00AM, and then 11:00AM rolled around and nothing happened yet. So, I called your mother on the phone by about 11:30AM and told her I didn't have any good news as of yet." She said, "Well it's still a little food left from last night. Come on home and get you something to eat." By this time the anticipation was eating me alive. "Come on Dad, tell me what happened next," I exclaimed. "Well, I tried to get up from the chair and something just pulled me back down. I felt really weak and tired. By 11:54AM, two cars pulled up in front of the shop. One of the cars had been all wrecked-up pretty bad in the front. A big stout man got out of the car and knocked on the shop door." With a boisterous voice he said, "I'm looking for the manager!" "I am the manager and my name is Mr. Moorer," dad replied. "Well, look here, you see my car is all torn up. Now how do you want to do this? I got an insurance check for $1,000.00 to take care of it. Do you want me to go up the street and cash it and give you ½ of it now, or do you want the whole grand now?"

I believed my Dad's story. The tears that filled the wells of his eyes and the goose bumps I felt reassured me of the sincerity and spirituality of the moment. That was certainly not the last testimony of God's greatness and deliverance that he shared with me. In his story, I saw how he was set up to believe God, even in the eye of despair. The same God that showed mercy and delivered on a promise back in 1979 was still available and able to deliver me in 1996.

That is why, for Christ's sake, I delight in weaknesses, in insults, in hardships, in persecutions, in difficulties. For when I am weak, then I am strong.

— 2 Corinthians 12:10

Understanding that God has to be the source of our strength, hope, and determination changes everything. As I completed each semester's course requirements, my transcript began to look decent. OCC offered to count my GMI course credits toward an associate's degree in engineering. I thought more about engineering coupled with my desire to focus on systems and organizational behavior.

From my brief stint in engineering at GM, I recalled that most engineers were also managers. All the plants' equipment was mechanized and any changes to a plant layout or its equipment fell under the category of project management. I was ready to bury the hatchet in terms of my academic pursuit of engineering. I now wanted to major in business management.

Many successful engineers pursue a business degree and begin to manage the function of engineering in their respective industries. I felt that I had an underlying understanding of engineering.

I was set up to pursue an entirely new track. The time had come to reapply for admission into GMI. My previous failures gave me a renewed vision and direction the following year. Would I end up back at GM in some capacity? If GM wouldn't be my corporate sponsor, then who would? Would I be able to catch up and graduate on time? I didn't have all the answers to any of these questions. I did know that I was taking God back to GMI with me this time. The baggage of worry and frustration was unloaded. I trusted that God would take care of my parents, the shop, and ordain my steps as I pursued the new track.

Chapter 7 – Stronger than Before

The Vice President of Academic Affairs made the terms of re-entry very clear and precise. The 'GMI Uniform Provisional Readmission Agreement' (UPRA) articulated all the requirements and stipulations of re-entry. The course work requirement consisted of the successful completion of no more than five courses. The course-load was supposed to be between 16 and 20 credit hours. As described in the UPRA, *"these courses are intended to demonstrate that the student has corrected the problems that led to the dismissal…"*

I read the contract from top to bottom with special emphasis on the *"performance requirement."* It read as follows: *"The student must achieve a term GPA equal to or greater than 85% with no individual course grade less than 77%."* In addition, I was required to make regularly scheduled visits to my academic advisor throughout the term. As for course selections, I selected four courses for a total of 16 credit hours. Statistics, Systems Analysis & Design, Financial Accounting, and Microeconomics were my courses of choice.

The load was perfect. I greatly enjoyed the three quantitative courses and the information systems course. All four professors were easy to approach and always available. I was equally impressed with all of them and their ability to articulate course subject-matter clearly and succinctly. I felt the pleasant difference between 16 and 23 credit hours. I had much more time to grasp each of the courses' concepts and to fully prepare for assessments.

In most academic institutions, 12 credit hours are needed to be considered a full-time student. GMI's requirements seemed to be higher in every statistical category excluding "intramural sports". Speaking of which, I made the time to reacquaint myself with a nice physical regimen of exercise, rest, and good nutrition. Most importantly, I started visiting a local church. I also commuted home every other weekend for church service. Overall the 'dismissal' was good for me.

> *"Come to me, all you who are weary and burdened, and I will give you rest. Take my yoke upon you and learn from me, for I am gentle and humble in heart, and you will find rest for your souls. For my yoke is easy and my burden is light."*
>
> — Matthew 11:28-30

Rest aids us in having a refreshed and a renewed vision. In your studying, cramming, and pursuit of success never underestimate the importance of a solid physical and spiritual regiment. The university's administration had invested heavily in the building of a new state-of-the-art full-service recreation center. The campus had changed drastically in a year. There were plenty of new faces in the student body.

Initially, I was a summer start back in 1994. As a restart, I began in the fall 1996 term. I was back in the dormitory. On the night before classes began, one of my best friends found my room and knocked on the door.

Ernest was brilliant then and still is today. He was attending for consecutive semesters while looking for a new corporate sponsor. We studied together every night. He had an incredible work ethic and a knack for the sciences. On most occasions, we entertained ourselves by watching Martin Lawrence's nationally televised sitcom: "*Martin.*" I found myself having light-hearted laughter and experiencing more joy on campus than ever before.

I felt that I had a commitment to do something for God. He had truly done so much for me. My academic studies came with ease. By midterm exams' week, I was flying high. The academic teachings and world of business management had a greater allure than ever before. In microeconomics, I was interested in the "why"/rationale behind supply and demand. Some of the economic constructs of natural resources, scarcity, and regional distribution were clear and self-explanatory.

The various connotations of economics fascinated me the most. Professor Ioannatos explained that economics is "the study of how wealth is created and distributed. Furthermore, the economy is the system that answers those two questions." In view of engineering and automobile design, production, and distribution, the terms were readily applicable to the microeconomic landscape of metropolitan Detroit. Factory workers and executives don't live in the same communities nor do they have the same consumption patterns. One lifestyle isn't better or of greater value than the next in intrinsic terms.

However, it was so enlightening for me to grasp and understand at age 20 that "incomes" determine "outcomes" in an academically illustrative manner. My business professors were imparting knowledge, understanding, and wisdom upon me in a major way. This awakening reminded me of my days in Dr. Sobol's OB course at OCC.

I believe that I began to excel so greatly partly because the material sparked my passions and intellectual interests. Systems analysis and design proved to be the gateway to my new path. Dr. Agarwal, my information systems instructor, was a first-year professor at the college, and he was new to the teaching profession.

New professors are often slightly more lenient and flexible than the seasoned tenured/senior faculty members. During his lectures, he periodically asked us to share with him how he could better explain the material. He was a young professor with a modest level of industry experience. His professional and academic background was quite inspiring. He and Dr. Sobol really made me start considering a future career in higher education.

I didn't emulate or covet their success or lifestyles. Their unique abilities to impart knowledge and leave a lasting intellectual impression inspired me the most. I knew that I wanted to shape lives and minds in a similar manner someday. Was I getting ahead of myself? *"This was a college flunkout we're talking about here."*

My academic advisor reminded me periodically of the seriousness of the probationary status. We chatted frequently about my progress, family-life, and future plans for the new semester. Our chats seemed like formality after a while. I knew that I was there to stay until the completion of the Bachelor of Science in Management degree program.

Others were not so easily convinced of the merit and veracity of my new track. Whispers swarmed that students who pursue management are academically inferior to engineering students. One of the most creative analogies relates to "pre-med students" who change majors and decide to pursue "philosophy". I didn't know if I had to contend directly with these notions. Do you find yourself challenged to contend with negative stereotypes and mental groupings? If you do, I want to offer a word of advice. People will always find categorical rankings and groupings to compare themselves and each other.

Abraham Maslow, a well-noted behavioral scientist, described five basic needs in his theory of motivation. The needs for affiliation, socialization, and self-esteem come to mind in this discussion. Unfortunately, many people assess their own value or self-worth relative to their estimate of others' value, or the value that others place on them. In the pecking order of engineering students, there is a multitude of classifications. Graduates are often assessed by the rank of their alma mater and the field of engineering that they pursue.

These categories of classifications are almost prevalent in all aspects of life, levels of achievement, and material wealth or gain. This is common even in the purchase of a dream car. Why did you get that color? What year is it? What's the MPG? Do you think they are going to change the body-style soon? Was it garage-kept? How many miles do you have on it by now? This host of questions is often followed by even more subtle comparisons and inquiries. There are some people who want to place doubt in your head about "who" you are and "where" you are headed. It is a true sign that they are unsure about who they are and which direction(s) they are headed in.

After a long evening of studying, I ran into one of the admissions recruiters in the cafeteria. I remembered him from previous semesters. He wanted to catch up and exclaimed that he was glad to see me on campus again. With a firm handshake and a seemingly sincere grin, he asked, "Cleamon, you made it back in, huh? How are classes coming along?" I was really glad to see him. "Things are great; I'm looking to major in management now. But I still want to be an engineer, just in a managerial capacity someday."

He began to shake his head and walk a short distance away. To my dismay, he returned with a broom and boldly extended it to me. "Take this! Because you might as well sweep floors if you think that you are going to succeed as a management major." I didn't know how to respond. There is a great honor in cleaning, but I didn't understand his point. I was brought up to believe that there was no form of labor beneath me. Thus, I can see the virtue of any meaningful occupation.

What was his motivation? He may've felt justified and correct in his assumption. What was his frame of reference? Obviously, he didn't think that my efforts would be worthwhile. He also didn't provide any scientific results to support his daunting prognosis. He just continued to say "… don't do it; you're making a big mistake."

My newfound success and passion felt far from being a mistake. In fact, my steps were beginning to feel ordained.

> *The LORD is the strength of his people, a fortress of salvation for his anointed one.*
>
> — Psalm 28:8

Those types of remarks were still burdensome. However, my real burdens had been lifted. Please don't wear the burdens of your doubters when God delivers you and is in the process of transforming you. In reality, they're doubtful of the power of God. And of course, God doubters will never reach their full potential. By the end of the semester, I was making plans to register for a new load of courses.

I went into final exams' week with a prayer, exercise, rest, and a good meal. There was no need to write my professors, *"This Is Why I Messed Up Memos"* on the back-side of exam papers. After all the scores were tallied, I finished the term with close to a 90% GPA. To my surprise, I received an official letter from the provost. Oh how the tone, content, and pitch of this letter differed from the "academic dismissal" communiqué. It read as follows:

> *Dear Mr. Moorer,*
>
> *Congratulations! You were successful in meeting the Provisional Readmission Agreement for the Fall 1996 term.*
>
> *As a result of your academic performance, you are now admitted as a Management degree seeking student.*
>
> *Please continue to seek the necessary help or guidance when needed to help keep you in good academic standing...*

I was back to stay this time, much stronger than before.

Statistics I:	88 (B+)
Systems Analysis & Design:	85 (B)
Financial Accounting:	91 (A-)
Microeconomics	87 (B)

Credits attempted: 16   *Credits earned: 16*

Never give up in your pursuits. A detour or change of track can be a form of divine intervention. Remember that God is the author and finisher of your faith.

> *Even youths grow tired and weary, and young men stumble and fall; but those who hope in the LORD will renew their strength. They will soar on wings like eagles; they will run and not grow weary, they will walk and not be faint.*
>
> — Isaiah 40:30-31

Chapter 8 – Victory Sensed but Unseen

1997

How much further was my faith going to take me? My degree-seeking student status was affirmed and reinstated. Failure was behind me. It wasn't a distant memory, because I thought about it often. Yet, I decided to continue moving forward. Upon returning to school for the next term my academic advisor notified me that I was due to receive a surprising accolade. I was placed on the Provost's List.

The Provost's List is for students who showed drastic improvement between semesters. Best of all, the list was displayed in the hall near the Registrar's Office for all to see. It would've been a really great testimony for other students only if they knew what I went through the prior year. But I still didn't feel comfortable elaborating or giving details about my previous failure.

Was I a hostage of my past? In hindsight, I believe that I was. When and if you are a hostage of your past, please try to let it go. If you don't let it go, you'll find yourself in unnecessary bondage. In addition, by withholding your testimony, you may keep others in bondage longer than they have to be.

So if the Son sets you free, you will be free indeed.

– John 8:36

In your attempts to move forward remember to help to bring others forward with you. I found myself more confident and exuberant than ever before. I experienced a true tale of going from worst to first. In order to make up for lost time, I successfully pursued 20 or more credit hours from that term forward.

My advisor was confident that I could handle a course-load of five or six classes each term. The business management curriculum increased in difficulty and complexity at each new level. I wondered if I would miss the academic course work of pursuing an engineering degree.

Although I had foregone the opportunity at OCC to get the associate's degree in engineering, I still thought like an engineer. After getting back into good student status, I was confident that I could do almost anything.

My new corporate relations manager understood that I wanted to go back either to GM or to another Fortune 500 corporation. I knew that I needed God's favor. Which Fortune 500 employer would accept me with a transcript like mine? My reaffirmed confidence still didn't outweigh my fear of the negative view that others may have had of me. My transferred courses from OCC were denoted as transfer credits earned. However, the grades were not calculated into my GPA. The failing scores were still configured into my GPA.

> *You will not have to fight this battle. Take up your positions; stand firm and see the deliverance the LORD will give you, O Judah and Jerusalem. Do not be afraid; do not be discouraged. Go out to face them tomorrow, and the LORD will be with you.*
>
> — 2 Chronicles 20:17

I believe that God often delivers us when we realize that we can't reach promise on our own. I didn't know which firm would be interested in hiring me. However, I wanted to be at a very profitable one. But I was willing to walk into any door that God opened for me.

My corporate relations manager worked diligently to place me. But by the end of the term, I still didn't have a job. I went back home to Detroit for the work term rotation. I brainstormed and prayed for direction as I looked for job opportunities.

The biggest challenge was to gain a position that would enable me to earn the co-op credits needed to graduate from GMI. My job at the shoe store didn't qualify, unless it was in a management capacity. My parents' business also was disqualified from the available choices.

One of my childhood friends told me that our grade-school counselor, Mr. Gardner, was now the Principal of Parker. I called and made an appointment to meet with him to see if there were any job openings at the school. When he made the time to meet with me, he asked, "So, you want to come back here to help us out?" I always admired him. Mr. Gardner expressed that he saw potential in me from my early beginnings. I replied, "In any way that I possibly can."

I was officially on a new track. He hired me to help maintain the school's computer network and to assist with instructing children on the use of computer applications. He intended for the position to be temporary until something better came along.

I was very content. It was an extraordinary opportunity to give back. The Board of Education only allowed him to pay me minimum-wage because the position was not approved in advance. I didn't do the math on the wages. I was thankful to God for His mighty hand of deliverance.

Humility is a vital virtue. I meet young people from time to time who boldly tell me that they won't and can't work for minimum-wage. The wage itself is not important. God measures our stewardship with what He blesses us with. How do you spend your money? What is important and necessary for you to purchase? Have you made a clear distinction between desires and needs? Which needs do your purchases satisfy? I was blessed to still be able to live with my parents during the work-terms.

Every good and perfect gift is from above, coming down from the Father of the heavenly lights, who does not change like shifting shadows.

— James 1:17

During the second week at Parker, I received a call for a job interview from the regional phone company. The phone interview went very well. Soon thereafter, I was brought in for a face-to-face interview. A week later, the company made me an offer too good to refuse. I screamed to the top of my lungs, *"Thank you Jesus!"* However, I was attached to the school kids and my position at Parker.

Mr. Gardner explained to me that he felt that my heart was in the right place. "Cleamon, give back when you really have something to give back. Don't forget us and where you came from. You have to move forward and do what's best for you right now." This closing interview was the best yet. Working downtown at the phone company as a manager in an engineering capacity was beyond what I dreamed of.

The roles and responsibilities of this position were also above my expectations. I was hired to develop a mechanized system for the five-state region. My manager explained that the process could easily take several years to complete. The system needed to connect engineers and technical support staff members in the operation of monitoring and rectifying service issues.

First, I had to learn the current process, systems, tasks, and roles of all users of the proposed system. Secondly, I needed to design, test, and create a system. Lastly, I believed the biggest challenge would be to implement and train employees on the proper use of the system.

Wow! Graduation was two years away. I would be able to dedicate four work-terms, which was equivalent to one calendar year to this project. I believed that if I developed the system successfully, then I would be offered a full-time position upon graduation.

The new track enabled me to learn quickly. The data engineering center was a perfect place to learn telephony. After three months, dial-tone, 3-way conference calling, and call-waiting were no longer mysteries. I understood how the phone system worked for local and long-distance services.

The data administration center in Detroit was full of women except for me and one other gentleman. All 21 employees including my boss looked at me as a son. Some of the employees took the responsibility of trying to groom me for success. It was unsolicited but appreciated. I believe that they felt I was the solution to many of the department's information systems related problems. Many of them often expressed that they wanted to see me graduate and run up the corporate ladder.

Their support and cooperation made it easier for me to do my job and to fulfill the ultimate goal of system development. I scheduled and broke each of the project's tasks into smaller parts. I always wanted to appear to be busy, deliberate, and diligent in addressing each task assigned to me.

My supervisor expressed her concern that I worked quickly and quietly. She admonished, "You don't write anything down. I want to look at your notes when you are away and when you go back to school." I didn't feel comfortable with adhering to that request. I wanted to protect my intellectual contributions. But it is very important to be an engaging team member in any work group or department.

I decided to let my guards down and share more of my insights and details of my progress. But I made sure to keep copies and back-up digital files of all of my contributions. By the end of the work-term, my supervisor and I had a good working relationship. We were both equally committed to developing the system. This was my most progressive work rotation yet. I was really glad that things hadn't worked out at GM. However, God proved very faithful all along in blessing me to be there for that particular season.

There was no way possible to be prepared for what awaited me when I returned to school the following term. During the fourth week of the term, it was very difficult for me to see the board from anywhere in the classroom. I asked several of my classmates to allow me to copy their notes.

I couldn't understand what happened to my eyesight. Was this a result of the tireless hours of reading and studying? The ophthalmologist diagnosed me with severe cataracts. I was born with them, but they increased over the years drastically. My vision was almost like looking through a cloudy glass of water.

I was diagnosed as being legally blind. It was curable. But what can't God cure? I was still scared. Throughout my childhood, I grew out of allergies, asthma, chicken-pox, and even a bout with meningitis. I had personally experienced God's healing power. However, this was different, I needed surgery immediately. God met me and the surgeons on the operating table. Even when the anesthesia grew less effective during the procedure, I wasn't overwhelmed by the pain.

> *At that very time Jesus cured many who had diseases, sicknesses and evil spirits, and gave sight to many who were blind.*
>
> – Luke 7:21

The recovery process went smoothly as planned. I didn't know how bad my eyesight really had been. I never saw colors so brightly before. I literally and figuratively began to see life much more clearly. My faith in God had grown drastically and my vision was close to "20-20"in both eyes.

Gone were the days of looking at God as Santa Claus. I experienced his healing power first-hand. I was now a college senior and graduation was vastly approaching. There was nothing that could stop me at that point. Or was there?

1999

Systems analysis and design afforded me the opportunity to travel frequently across the company's five-state region. I was a student who was living like an executive. I traveled to Chicago and Indianapolis to consult with engineers, planners, and technicians.

The company secured limousine transportation to and from the airport. That lifestyle was easy to get used to. I stayed in five-star hotels in each city and dined at the finest restaurants. I worked very long hours and days during my work-terms. Even during my last two school-terms, I commuted from Flint to Detroit to work several days a week on the project.

My supervisor told me that, even though I worked during the last school-term, I wasn't supposed to get paid for the hours worked. She exclaimed, "All of that work was extra; you weren't supposed to get direct deposits during that time!" This did not make any sense to me at all. I replied, "So, I was supposed to make the commute and work for free?" She responded furiously by saying, "Yes! The completion of your degree is contingent upon the success of this system. So it was your responsibility to do whatever it took to make it happen at your own expense." I couldn't believe this. I designed a system that would potentially save the company millions of dollars. But I was being treated as though I stole something.

She decided that the only solution was to make me work the entire term without pay. Her manager agreed to it. So it was settled. I had no recourse but to push further. I explained the situation to my dad. As usual, he knew exactly what to say. "Son, it seems as though you got your hand caught in the lion's mouth," he responded. Lions and lionesses were too pleasant of images; instead I envisioned gorillas and bears. He went further to elaborate on his analogy by saying, "When your hand is in the lion's mouth don't try to snatch it out. Rub his head and ease it out." I fully understood his analogy.

bless those who curse you, pray for those who mistreat you.
— Luke 6:28

I was facing another difficult time. How can you be nice to those who are taking full advantage of you? This was much different from flunking-out, losing my job, and a temporary loss of sight. My boss was actually taking what I earned away from me. I felt helpless, but still determined. I'd overcome so much. Victory was sensed, but yet unseen. The new challenge set before me was to work harmoniously at least 90 days without a paycheck.

But he said to me, "My grace is sufficient for you, for my power is made perfect in weakness." Therefore I will boast all the more gladly about my weaknesses, so that Christ's power may rest on me.
— 2 Corinthians 12:9

Chapter 9 – Answered Prayer

You give me your shield of victory, and your right hand
sustains me; you stoop down to make me great.

– Psalm 18:35

I was not completely broke. My work-study position provided me with enough money to commute between work and school. I tried not to dwell on what had happened. God showed me that He was still with me several times during this period.

The cafeteria was on the 12th floor of the telecom building. I would often go up there in the late afternoon to take a break and think about the future. I could always faintly hear gospel music as soon as I got off of the elevator. There was a cleaning lady's workstation next to the elevators. She usually greeted me as she continued to complete her daily assignments. One day she introduced herself as Mother Matthews and invited me into her work area.

Her work space was very peaceful and clean. It was about 5' x 8' in dimension. The walls were filled with scriptural references and angelic images. She asked if it was okay to pray with and for me. Following her prayer, she explained to me that she could see the presence of the Lord upon my countenance. Mother Matthews told me that I was special, and she expressed a belief that God had great works for me to perform throughout my life. Her consultation eased my burden, and I made regular visits to Mother Matthews' workstation at least twice a week.

Who has God sent to talk and pray with and for you? Has He sent you to pray for anyone? Don't harden your heart to the blessed words of wise people. Spiritual support and nourishment are far greater than our material wants and desires. You will be able to discern and understand the voice of God as you spend time seeking Him. Also, be sure to accompany yourself with Godly people, especially during your time of need.

> *For where two or three come together in my name, there am I with them.*
>
> — Matthew 18:20

God continued to assure me of His presence physically and spiritually during that stretch. Michigan winters are known to be very fierce. Frigid temperatures often bring ice, sleet, and snow to many of the highways, roads, and overpasses.

On one particular winter morning, I was commuting to Flint and lost complete control of my car. My 1995 Mustang was not prepared for the ice that day. The age-old saying of *"don't fight the wheel when sliding on ice,"* resonated half-way through my losing battle. I barely missed hitting the guard rail by two or three feet. The car's uncontrollable spinning and sliding left the rear end of it hanging off of a cliff overlooking a small river.

He saved me again, in spite of my shortcomings and the thoughts of many others. God decided to rescue me. I couldn't bring myself to devise a false maverick story of how I avoided tragedy.

> *Whoever tries to keep his life will lose it, and whoever loses his life will preserve it.*
>
> — Luke 17:33

I was beginning to realize that I had to turn everything over to God. You can't do anything worthwhile without the powerful hand of God. In this busy age of online classes, social networking, and telecommuting many people have placed their prayer lives on auto-pilot. All of our technological advancements of instant messaging and Wi-Fi still don't yield the immediate deliverance that comes from calling on the name of Jesus.

From that day on, I started to talk and pray to God more during my commutes. As the weather changed and the school-term came to end, I grew more and more anxious about the days ahead. My thesis advisor put the finishing touches on his assessment and critique of my final project.

I implemented the new system at the beginning of the year. All the travel, work, and sacrifice had truly paid off. I had worked with many engineers, managers, and technicians across the region during the previous two years. Most importantly, I had an underlying understanding of how the telecommunications industry worked and functioned as a whole.

My supervisor's manager called to thank me for all of my contributions to the department, the business unit, and the organization. He went on to offer me an official full-time position as an equipment engineer. The position was in Chicago. I asked about a starting bonus or a relocation assistance package. He replied, "Well, I waived your starting bonus to apply it to the monies that you still owed the company." I tried to reply with a valid defense. "I've been off of payroll for three months. I didn't believe that I owed anything in the first place. Wasn't working for free for three months enough?"

His response seemed as though he was well prepared for this discussion. "No, from our calculations it's still not enough. If you want the position, it is imperative that you are here in two weeks to start on March 26th. Furthermore, I don't have any recommendations as to how you will afford to relocate."

My prayer was answered. *"Dear God, please make me an engineer."* It was only three and a half years prior that I had knelt on the floor of my apartment and prayed that prayer to God. It had truly come to pass upon my acceptance of the position. The obstacles ahead didn't bear any dismay or gloom to the joy, peace, and deliverance that I experienced.

> *Ask and it will be given to you; seek and you will find; knock and the door will be opened to you.*
> — Matthew 7:7

I knew that God would get me there. I needed some recent pay stubs to lease an apartment in Chicago. Of course I did not have any due to being taken off of payroll three months earlier. The YMCA was the best and seemingly only option.

However, when the administrator at the 'Y' read my official letter of offer, she responded by saying, "You're going to make way too much money to live here at the Y". What was going on? I was so close to destiny. Have you ever found yourself at the brink of destiny while facing huge obstacles? Just remember that God is not surprised or outdone by any of our challenges.

Could it be that they offered me a job, but didn't want or expect for me to take it? Maybe they didn't want me to be able to take the position. I had to go back to "*who*" I asked for the job in the first place. It wasn't about them. It was all about staying and being on the path that God set for me. Be sure to stay on the course that God has set for you, regardless of circumstances, forces, and opposition: Do stay on the course!

I tell you the truth, if anyone says to this mountain, 'Go, throw yourself into the sea,' and does not doubt in his heart but believes that what he says will happen, it will be done for him.   – Mark 11:23

It was clear to me that God was with me, and that He was going to get me where I needed to be. After several days of searching the virtual classifieds, I stumbled upon a rental ad that fit my budget. I could board a room in what appeared to be a half-way house on Chicago's north-side. It was close to commuter trains, decent, clean, and most of all affordable. The property manager required a $150.00 deposit to move in.

I'd relocated to Chicago the weekend before I was due to begin work. I left everything and everyone that I knew to pursue my life-long hope and dream of becoming an engineer.

If you remain in me and my words remain in you, ask whatever you wish, and it will be given you.

– John 15:7

Chapter 10 – Living the Hope and Dream

Chicago is only about 300 miles west of Detroit. But it was a big move for me. My mother cooked a delicious meal before my departure. We prayed, embraced, talked, and said our goodbyes. My father made sure to remind me that the same God that watched over me in Detroit and Flint would also take care of me in Chicago. I believed that and I was encouraged to charter new waters. Eleanor Roosevelt said it best, *"You gain strength, courage, and confidence by every experience in which you really stop to look fear in the face. You are able to say to yourself, 'I lived through this horror. I can take the next thing that comes along."*

I stopped by to see Reggie and his mom on my route to the highway. Saying goodbye to them was a bittersweet experience. His mother always made her house and kitchen a home away from home for me. I knew that I was going to miss them dearly.

We had grown to be like a family over the years. Reggie solemnly said, "I don't want to see you go, but I know that you got to move on and do better for yourself." This was a tough moment for me. Reggie and I were like brothers. We watched each other mature and evolve. He befriended me during the same time that Julian went to the Army. We vowed to stay in touch.

A man of many companions may come to ruin, but there is a friend who sticks closer than a brother.

— Proverbs 18:24

I didn't turn away from the past. I wanted to be sure to use my past as a guide into the future. It is imperative that you use the joy and sorrow of your past to embrace the future. Some people use the cliché, "You know where you have been, but you don't know where you are going." I offer the rebuttal that this may be true, but I do know *who* is going to meet me where I'm going. And, He knows my beginning and my end. You have to trust God every step of the way.

On my first day of work, the staff coordinator introduced me to all of my new colleagues and I began orientation. I had worked with many of the engineers on my team during the system development process. A boisterous fan of the system shouted from his cubicle, "…so how does it feel to work on the system that you designed from the other side of it?" Bob was both a good engineer and mentor. I replied, "Bob, it is a dream come true, thanks for your support!" It was surreal. I was officially an engineer and a part of the team, but not just any part of the team. I felt vital to the inner workings of the business unit.

I was assigned central offices and equipment to maintain. I monitored traffic, utilization, and efficiency on a vast array of telephone equipment. The telecommunications industry speaks its own language. There is an acronym for everything. It is a truly a different language. However, I was prepared to learn the new language and to meet the goals and objectives of our department.

I was on the fast track. I was 23 years old and working as an engineer and project manager in one of the nation's most dominant telecommunications companies. Many of my colleagues were supportive and helpful. Success is never achieved alone. You must form alliances at each level. It is not about likes and dislikes.

High performance is garnered through a shared commitment to win as a team. I was quite the object of diversity in my business unit. The factors of race, age, and socio-economic background distinguished me from most of my colleagues. As I looked at upper management, I saw less diversity at the top of the company. I recall thinking, *"I am young, black, and from Detroit, how will I be received as I climb the corporate ladder?"* The Bible offers a passage for that type of thinking.

But you are a chosen people, a royal priesthood, a holy nation, a people belonging to God, that you may declare the praises of him who called you out of darkness into his wonderful light.

– 1 Peter 2:9

God knew that I would be young and black in that era and on that path before he ordained it. Please keep in mind that no matter how different you look, you aren't deficient. Simply because you don't see many people who look like you where you are going, doesn't mean that you should turn back. Don't wait for an invitation to possess what is rightfully yours.

As you plan for the future and begin to walk into your destiny, please remember the importance of *p*reparation, *o*pportunity, and the *w*ill of God. I refer to this combination as *POW*, then add *e*nter and *r*eceive. Now you have the *POWER*. *POW* strikes a blow on the door of fate and destiny. You have to be humble, strong, and patient in your quest for *POWER*. Remember to be *f*aithful and to express and extend *u*nlimited *l*ove to everyone. That sounds like a *POWERFUL* strategy to move forward.

But the meek will inherit the land and enjoy great peace. – Psalm 37:11

My life had become peaceful and victorious. I was successful and eager to achieve more. Within the first six months of being in Chicago, I bought my first home. The communities and highway systems had become easier to navigate. I began attending a local church in my community and was poised to get to higher heights in Christ.

I invited my parents up to visit me and see my new home. They were overjoyed with my success. On the first night of their weekend visit, my dad came out of the bedroom to have coffee with me in the kitchen. For the first time ever, he was sitting at my kitchen table. We caught up on all the recent and latest events. However, women were the main theme of his conversation. Particularly, he wanted to know how I had been spending my social time.

All throughout high school and college I had several girlfriends. None of the relationships were long-term or ordained by God to be more than platonic. Through all of my previous non-platonic relationships, I truly learned more about myself, and what I wasn't looking for in a potential spouse. I had made mistakes in this area that aren't worth mentioning. I think my father sensed all of that. He went into a discussion pertaining to how everything in my life was going well, but I was missing my soul-mate. I concurred. So as usual we prayed. Following the prayer, he prophesied that I would meet my future wife within 30 days.

Granted my father was gifted and anointed, but this was the first time that I experienced him being "chronological" and precise with prophecy. *"Come on, Dad, how do you know that?"* With great certainty, he responded, "…because God just brought it to me and told me to tell you." He advised me to keep living a clean life in the meanwhile and expect my queen. I began to praise and thank God and believe that He would send her to me soon.

Two weekends later, some men from the church that I grew up in were in Chicago for a conference. One of the brothers agreed to join me for lunch. We needed to get some gas before our departure. While I was fueling my car, I saw her all at once. She was at the fuel station window paying the attendant. My heart began to beat really fast. I was getting all shook up. I knew that I had to make acquaintance with her. *"But at a gas station?"* Nice going Dad, what a vivid prophecy!

I didn't want to appear strange by approaching her at the fuel pump. There was another young lady waiting in the car for her. They appeared to be as opposite as night and day. I wasn't dressed like a peddler, but I did not want her to believe that my approach or coming on to her was routine. Time was of the essence. I had to seal the deal and close in on my destiny. As the gifted recording artist K'Jon sang, "My ship had finally come."

"Rico, we're going to follow them!" As I began to drive forward, she drove her car in the same path, and lowered her window to ask me for directions to the freeway. It was fate. My car still had Michigan license plates on it. I wasn't the best person to ask for directions. But I gladly pulled to the side to be as helpful as I possibly could be.

I briefly explained to Rico the urgency of this encounter. He agreed to communicate with the passenger while I operated. I put my best forward and strutted toward her like a proud peacock. All jokes aside, I was very serious about making my move. "Operation Buttercup" was in full effect. Nicole and I have now been happily married for 14 years. She is my buttercup, my 'cherie-amore', best friend, and life-partner. God has blessed our marriage exceedingly and abundantly well. We are now the proud parents of four boys.

> *He who finds a wife finds what is good and receives favor from the LORD.*
>
> — Proverbs 18:22

I was living a dream. The promised-land experience was worth all the anguish and turmoil that it took to fulfill it. My joy was unspeakable. But when I returned to Detroit to visit my parents, I saw that they weren't doing well.

C & M Collision had seen its best days. My father was 72, and he was still trying to operate a labor-intensive business. He had just undergone a major undisclosed surgical procedure. Business closure can be very difficult for a sole proprietor. Without knowing all the details of their distress, I understood that they needed my help.

Nicole and I offered my parents an opportunity to move to Chicago. We were expecting our first child and wanted more living space. God blessed us to purchase another home around the corner from the first one. I didn't want my parents to have to worry about making ends meet anymore. My father's pride was softened by his gratitude and God's hand of deliverance.

> *Give, and it will be given to you. A good measure, pressed down, shaken together and running over, will be poured into your lap. For with the measure you use, it will be measured to you.*
>
> — Luke 6:38

This was the start of many new beginnings and closure to old chapters. When I faced great adversity at GMI, I never thought that I would see days like this. Being happily married, awaiting the birth of my first child, and being blessed to retire and relocate my parents were truly supernatural feats.

I prayed for wisdom much earlier in my life. Gaining wisdom doesn't come by osmosis. You have to experience life and all that comes with it. At this point, my career had truly taken off. I had worked to get into upper-middle management and was in the process of pursuing graduate school.

My material wealth had grown beyond my initial expectations in a very short period of time. I bought a couple of classic Cadillacs. Great things were happening at an alarming rate. What could God possibly have in store for me next?

Chapter 11 – The Calling

My ascension into upper-middle management had become a reality. Corporate success was a great feeling. But once again, I wanted and needed more. The company offered managers 100% tuition pre-payment to attend any college or university of their choice. I felt that I had to take full advantage of that opportunity. I had planned to return to school before I moved to Chicago.

The Master of Business Administration (MBA) was beginning to be considered by most the gold stamp for managers who aspired to get into a top-management position. However, I had PhD aspirations. I learned from my previous failure that it was imperative to go a step above and beyond the current expectations. What is considered to be acceptable by most decision makers today can easily become insufficient by those very same individuals tomorrow.

Some universities allow some candidates to enter PhD programs without having a master's degree. I completed a thesis project at the undergraduate level. Thus, I viewed master's degree work as a formality. My local search for PhD programs yielded only a handful of options.

Benedictine University offered a unique PhD program in Organizational Development (OD). I researched the distinction between OD and OB. I concluded that I wanted to understand both organizational diagnostic tools and the psycho-social behaviors of organizational stakeholders.

The directors of Benedictine University's PhD program welcomed my attempt to enter the PhD program, but they clearly suggested that I first pursue and attain a master's degree in business, OD, or OB. So, I decided to enroll as a full-time OB graduate, degree-seeking student. I attended classes during the evenings, early mornings, and weekends.

I was driven by my corporate success and my desire to have unlimited career options. Graduate school was a natural fit into my schedule and aspirations. My classes were taught by seasoned professionals and emerging scholars. I found myself in class six days out of the week for most of the quarters.

Writing papers and analyzing case studies was the primary focus of the OB program. Most of my classmates were consultants, managers, or human resources professionals from large or medium-sized organizations. Many of them were most collegial and open to learning from one another. Grad school was different in that it was optional and much more comprehensive and intuitive than undergraduate studies.

In hindsight, undergraduate studies seemed so pragmatic. The goal was often to learn the right formula or theory and to perform well on a quiz or exam. In graduate school, I began to question theories and their applicability or resolve when applied to real-world situations.

Several of the courses were arranged as seminars and weekend workshops. In most of the OB courses, students were directed to work in groups and to work remotely to develop strategies to address simulated organizational issues. I enjoyed the opportunities to debate my rationale or position on topics, whether it was congruent or incongruent with my peers' ideas.

My passion for OB was reignited. I thrived and excelled in the courses pertaining to process consultation, business process redesign, group dynamics, and team-building. Best of all, I could apply my real-time learning to my team and projects at work. Within 11 months, I completed all the course requirements to earn a master's of science in Management and Organizational Behavior (MSMOB) degree. I completed my MBA six months later.

I enjoyed and thrived in the quantitative and analytical courses. Accounting, finance, managerial economics, operations, and statistics challenged and fine-tuned my problem-solving capabilities. Many of my fellow MBA classmates were not as equally interested in the *"soft-skills"* taught in the MSMOB curriculum. But I desired versatility and increased marketability. My MBA concentrations were Leadership and Management Consulting, both of which I aspired to utilize in my current and future prospective positions.

I was learning in school and at work. At times it seemed that I was doing more learning than working. Was all of this learning just for corporate success? That question challenged me and consumed many of my personal moments. Have you ever been interested and disinterested at the same time? For the first time in my life, I was excelling but also distracted by what appeared to be a higher calling.

This distraction was clear to many people around me. My general manager frequently sent us to industry training with our vendors and external partners. After several days of training and learning about new equipment and technologies, it was natural to build a rapport with new colleagues, classmates, and instructors.

One of my instructors was a seasoned and extremely intelligent middle-aged woman, by the name of Bea Petty. I will never forget Bea or her command of the technological subject-matter. She approached me during our lunch-break one day and said, "Cleamon, you seem so withdrawn from all of this technical information." I wanted to respond in a politically-correct manner. "No, I love it; it's great!" She divinely and empathetically responded, "… you can't fool me. This is just busy work for you. There are much greater things that you are destined to do in life. Just hang in there in the meanwhile."

Bea didn't know me personally. Why did she feel comfortable telling me this? What was I supposed to do with her proclamation? Even in the midst of great success, I felt that eventually there would be something different for me to do. Could it be that my purpose in life was far greater than being an engineer and an executive?

For we are God's workmanship, created in Christ Jesus to do good works, which God prepared in advance for us to do.

— Ephesians 2:10

What about you? Have you sought God and the elders in pursuit of your life's calling? Are you doing well, but desire to do even greater? My barometer for measuring how well I was doing had changed. Material gain, corporate success, and promotion had become less important. Some of my colleagues began to criticize my thirst for direction and fulfillment. *"You just don't know how good you got it."*

God spoke to me concerning my calling, one evening while I was in a managerial economics course. At the time, I was doing my normal doodling and practicing my pre-drafted "Dr." signatures. God's voice was faint but very distinctive and incomparable.

'I've taught you what you need to know to live perfectly. Now, you must travel the entire world and teach my people all about me."

When God calls you, you will know it, and you'll never be able to forget it. You will know that it is Him because the contents of His message are so different bat your plans.

> *My sheep listen to my voice; I know them, and they follow me.*
> − John 10:27

Consider the book of Jonah. Where did Jonah want to go? Where did God tell him to go? What happened?

I immediately excused myself from class and went to a payphone to call my parents. "Hello Momma, how are you? Is Dad still awake?" I was bubbling with excitement, confusion, and anxiety. "Here he is," she said as she handed him the phone. I told him what just happened in the classroom. "Well, it's not quite time yet. God is getting you ready. But it's coming soon. You have to start preparing yourself and paying closer attention to His voice."

At that point, I realized that my earthly father could only see and tell me so much about the future. I had to seek God for myself in order to understand how to proceed and what was to come. For some reason, I thought it was going to be easy to interpret, understand, and to fulfill my calling.

Several years prior, my father had a long-awaited discussion with me on my 21st birthday. He had often forewarned during my teen years that he would share something with me on my 21st birthday. I never knew what he had to share, but I had thought about it a great deal leading up to my birthday. My mother wouldn't give me any hints through the years.

"The night that you were conceived, God told me this: I have created a son in the womb of your wife. He will do everything that I intended for you to do. He will be one of the greatest prophets to walk the face of the earth excusing Christ Jesus. You are not to tell him until his 21st birthday. You are to raise him, protect him, and guide him in the direction that he should go."

I said, "Come on now, Dad, are you serious?" He responded, "Yes sir, Champ, I will never forget what he told me about you. I may not be around to see it, but it will come to pass." I didn't know what do with that prophecy back then. Four years later sitting in managerial economics, I still didn't have a clear vision of what do with the prophecy and the calling.

The merits of my father's prophecy; Mother Matthews' words; Bea's proclamation; and God's direct words to me served as the basis for why I felt that there were greater things for me to do. I wondered when and how? I worked so hard to become an engineer and a global service executive. My education was all grounded in business, engineering, and management. As I walked back into the classroom, I felt goose-bumps all over my body. I knew that the presence of the Lord was upon me.

The Spirit of the Lord is on me, because he has anointed me to preach good news to the poor. He has sent me to proclaim freedom for the prisoners and recovery of sight for the blind, to release the oppressed.

– Luke 4:18

I talked with Nicole in great length about the realities of my satisfaction-dissatisfaction with my current work situation. I was happy, for the most part, until I started to experience this unequivocal pull to move quicker down the path of destiny. She comforted me and assured me that God would make it clearer to us in due time and season.

We didn't know what to expect in the future. Would we have our own church? Would we become missionaries? Would our lives in some way, shape or form, become living ministries? It was clear to both of us that at some point we would have to pursue the work of God, which may have meant leaving corporate America.

We had tentative horizons of my departure from the company set for the distant future. I estimated that perhaps several years down the road, I would be ready to leave the company. We went as far as to calculate how much money we would have in the bank at that set time and what my job title or rank would be. Have you ever thought that you had it all figured out?

A faith-walk with God is like nothing that you will ever experience. It can force you to question everything and everyone that you've known. Our company was in the process of being acquired by another telecommunications giant. The merger of these companies was orchestrated to form the largest telecommunications company in the world. There were a lot of changes going on with management, positions, groups, and departments.

My team was going through a major overhaul. Some of my unit's leaders were granting employees transfers to other departments. My recent attainment of two master's degrees made me a threat to some of my colleagues and supervisors. I wasn't looking to replace anyone or to take anyone else's position. I simply wanted to capitalize on the full tuition prepayment benefit and to increase both my internal and external options for advancement.

The inter-organizational turmoil brought on by the merger coupled with tremendous discord in my business unit led me to do what many people considered the unthinkable. Big mergers often bring about uncertainty. Some managers feared that they may be fired or down-sized. My immediate supervisor's boss was the most intimidated by my academic and professional success. He launched an agenda to politically-assassinate my character, integrity, and work ethic. It seemed that he interpreted my ambition as an attempt to undermine the age-old bureaucratic paradigm that promotion should only be granted by tenure.

I sat down with him to discuss his tactics, my position, and the interdepartmental relations.

He wouldn't disclose any of his intentions or plans for me or others in the department. As I sat in his office, God spoke to me once again. This time His words were much fewer than on the day of calling. God told me, *"It's over."*

After close to ten years of corporate experience and the completion of three college degrees, I decided to resign from my upper middle management position at the world's largest telecommunications company.

> *but the world must learn that I love the Father and that I do exactly what my Father has commanded me. "Come now; let us leave.*
>
> – John 14:31

I needed the freedom to hear more from God how and where to proceed. And, of course I still needed to provide for my family.

2002

This was the start of a new and trying season for me. I started a new business venture titled Moorer Customer Care Solutions Consulting. I built upon my industry contacts and my education in management consulting to seek consulting opportunities. For 18 months, God worked with me as I tried to build a successful consulting firm. He had my full attention. It was truly a wilderness experience. I realized that even though I was a sole proprietor, God was really my boss. I often prayed and pondered,"...oh God, How are we going to pay the bills and secure contracts this month?"

In the process of launching and operating the new business, we rapidly depleted most of our savings. I had to sell my classic Cadillacs in order to keep things afloat. But God was not done speaking to my heart. I found myself making sacrifices and doing things that I didn't want to do to in order to provide for my family. At times, I second-guessed my decision to leave corporate America so soon. During a prayer one night, God gave me a theme and motto that I learned to live by.

"One often has to do what they have to do in order to do what they want to do; however, if you only do what you want to do, then you will never do what you have to do."

Several of my friends and acquaintances questioned my sanity. One of my closest friends from GMI candidly shared his unsolicited diagnosis and perception of my decision. "Man, you are so far off the road right now! My life is clear and straight. The road ahead of me is beautiful. But you are traveling through the trees and the wilderness. I hope it all works out for you somehow..."

I knew that my decision and that the fast track that I was on was contrary to the norm. Mocking, ridicule, and nay-saying is not your dish of choice during the uncertain times of your life. Have you ever made a move that placed you in a wilderness experience? Would you ever consider trusting God enough to do whatever He tells you to? You should embrace the wilderness for the following reasons:

- Abraham was in the *wilderness* because he was following God's instruction.
- David was in the *wilderness* because Saul wanted to kill him.
- Elijah was in the *wilderness* because he wanted to die; he wanted to die because he was unsuccessful.
- Jesus was in the *wilderness* to prepare for his ministry.
- Jonah was in the *belly of a whale* (equivalent to a wilderness experience) because of his disobedience.

All of these great men of God including the greatest Jesus Christ experienced the *"wilderness"* for different reasons. Wilderness experiences help us to get a full meaning of our lives. They help us to trust God undoubtedly. While in the wilderness, it should become clear to us that God has complete control of our lives. Last but not least, I believe that God uses the wilderness experience to prepare us for even greater works that He has planned for us to perform. I am so happy that I can share testimonies from my wilderness experiences with you now. When we were going through and seeking direction, we didn't know any of these tenets of the wilderness experience.

But most importantly, Nicole walked with me in the wilderness. She didn't act like Job's wife. We decided that we would not abort our struggling business, but we continued to wait on God to deliver us.

I actually began to appreciate some of the down-time between projects. I had time to fast, read my bible, and seek God in my office space. Our first-born was going on two years of age as God began to reveal Himself more and more to me. I was more concerned about his life and Nicole's life than my very own. At that very moment, I desperately wanted to advance out of the wilderness experience and into a favorable vision of fullness and spiritual prosperity.

Chapter 12 – Envisioning the future

Writing down a prayer request wasn't my original idea of bringing closure to my wilderness experience. The pastor of the church that I grew up in, Reverend Robinson, often led church members to write down their prayer requests and burn them before the Lord. I had many questions pertaining to that strategy. I didn't try it; but I tried something else that was really contrary to God's teachings.

During one of the most challenging moments of my wilderness experience, I was persuaded by a television commercial to call a 1-900 number to speak to a Psychic Reader. The *"reader,"* of course, knew absolutely nothing about me, my path, or journey. She asked several questions in an attempt to keep me on the phone to increase the charges of the call.

> *Dear friends, do not believe every spirit, but test the spirits to see whether they are from God, because many false prophets have gone out into the world.*

> – 1 John 4:1

God had always provided me with a credible and valid source to talk to and with during the darkest hours of my life. I needed to know what to pray for. Have you ever been lost for words in your prayer life? Is it always clear exactly what to pray for? At this juncture, I wanted the wilderness experience to be over. But I grew closer to God and learned so much that

I couldn't honestly say that I would never welcome another wilderness experience.

I uncovered the dishonesty and sin of palm reading and fortune-telling. Most importantly, I began to understand the significance of patience. My consulting practice had grown slow to non-existent. I considered making a return to corporate America. Several of my friends and colleagues provided job leads, suggestions, and recommendations. However, none of their prospects yielded a feasible opportunity.

I knew that God didn't lead me to that point to leave me. Once again, another woman of God began to speak wisdom into my life and situation. I met Mother Jones when I was a global service executive. Similar to Mother Matthews, she also took the time to share insights and revelations with me. I kept in touch with her following my resignation. During one of our phone conversations, she adamantly instructed, "Write down exactly what you want and need from God, believe it, and you will receive it."

I searched my heart, and came up with a list of what I truly desired. Somehow, it was easier to write down the ideas and desires than it was to speak them.

Then the LORD replied: "Write down the revelation and make it plain on tablets so that a herald may run with it. For the revelation awaits an appointed time; it speaks of the end and will not prove false. Though it linger, wait for it; it will certainly come and will not delay.

– Habakkuk 2:2-3

My list comprised the following:

- A position that will enable me to be a blessing to others.
- A commute to either downtown or within close driving proximity to my home.
- I want to be honored and respected for my value to the workplace.
- Lastly, a six-figure salary (at least $100,000 a year).

I prayed and went further to establish a covenant with God. I promised to testify about His mighty hand of direction and deliverance in my life to the entire world.

> *They will ask the way to Zion and turn their faces toward it. They will come and bind themselves to the Lord in an everlasting covenant that will not be forgotten.*

> — Jeremiah 50:5

An active prayer life of seeking God, obedience, and continuous reading of scripture offers God an amazing opportunity to lead and guide you. I began to realize this in the greatest form yet. It was obvious that I needed to secure a full-time position and use my consulting practice as a supplement or compliment to a day-job.

During the 14th month of my wilderness experience, God spoke to me and gave me very clear instructions.

"Get up; get on the computer and find a PhD program."

Most of my routine internet searches were focused on jobs or consulting opportunities. But this time, God was directing me to go back to school and not to work. How would school pay the bills? Wouldn't school create more expenses? Haven't I already completed enough school? You would've thought by then that I had enough of questioning God. Maybe I expected immediate delivery of the contents in my covenant. Never waste your time or energy questioning God's direction. Regardless of what you see or think, please remember that He knows all things.

> *For in the gospel a righteousness from God is revealed, a righteousness that is by faith from first to last, just as it is written: "The righteous will live by faith."*

> — Romans 1:17

I was discouraged by my earlier attempt to get into a PhD program. The directors of the PhD program at Benedictine University told me that

I needed to complete a master's degree first. After the completion of two master's degrees, I applied for entry into the PhD program.

The associate director of the program poignantly asked, "Cleamon, why do you want it?" I explained that I believed that it would strengthen my research capabilities and offerings as a consultant. I remembered to remind the committee that my pursuit of the PhD was what prompted me to enroll at that university in the first place.

She responded by saying, "Well, it doesn't guarantee more money. In fact, you're already accomplished enough. You're a consultant. You've been an engineer and executive. Plus, you already have two master's degrees. I don't believe that this is a really good fit for you."

This was supposed to be an interview. It took a terrible turn. I couldn't understand why the interview committee worked so greatly to discourage me. Have you ever been turned away by individuals in your pursuit of destiny? Should you retreat? Absolutely not... it should make you want the blessed object of your desire just that much more.

So months later, when God directed me to get on the computer and find a PhD program, I reflected on that previous encounter. He helped me to understand that I was still on the fast track and that their past rejection of me was meant to serve as a channel for me to seek Him in all of my pursuits.

I enjoyed training and developing employees in corporate settings. But my desire to enter the classroom as a lecturer grew more and more. Usually when people envision a college professor, an appearance similar to mine doesn't first come to mind. In addition, 'flunking-out' of college isn't a prerequisite for a scholastic career in higher education. I was an experienced engineer, manager, executive, and independent consultant, but I was also a 26 year-old black male. I knew that I would have to overcome many negative stereotypes in order to reach promise. The ideal professor in many people's eyes is an older, more experienced, seasoned, half-bald gentleman, who has a proud but weathered collection of cardigan sweaters. My journey and path seemed so peculiar. God laid the infrastructure to what was becoming an *uncommon path to professoriate.*

Don't let anyone look down on you because you are young, but set an example for the believers in speech, in life, in love, in faith and in purity.

— 1 Timothy 4:12

I followed God's directions. I found a PhD program on the internet. I later interviewed and was accepted into a doctorate of business administration (DBA) program at Argosy University. DBA programs that require a dissertation and comprehensive examinations are equivalent to PhD programs according to most universities' standards.

Argosy University was once the American Schools of Professional Psychology. Argosy's Business School was a completely new venture. I would've been skeptical about entering into an unknown non-traditional PhD/DBA program if God had not directed me to do so. Some of my colleagues and former professors scrutinized the merit of a new non-traditional doctorate program. Once again, at a very pivotal time in my life, I stayed on the path that God set before me.

If anyone chooses to do God's will, he will find out whether my teaching comes from God or whether I speak on my own.

— John 7:17

Shortly after entering into the DBA program, I began searching for teaching positions. There comes a point in time when an individual has to reposition his/her self to obtain what he/she desires. Repositioning was not a new intervention for me. I made the necessary changes to become a successful college student. In addition, the transformations from being an engineer, to a service executive, and then to an independent consultant required heightened levels of repositioning.

I believed that it was imperative to think like an academic. Whatever you want to achieve in life, you must begin with the appropriate mindset. I searched various virtual higher education job posting boards and websites to discover and navigate to and through potential opportunities.

The distant approach of surveying from afar wasn't enough for me. I wanted to get a sense of the distinctions between various colleges and universities. In addition, I was hopeful that God would give me a certain feeling of comfort or belonging when I physically set foot on a campus. So, I started visiting college campuses in the Chicago-land area, placing a specific emphasis on business faculty offices and teaching environments.

At several of the institutions, the deans of the business schools were available and did take some time to speak with me. Many of their demeanors and responses varied from cordial to overtly disinterested in my offer to apply to join the professoriate.

It seemed like a private society, for the most part. Many of the faculty members at each institution had graduated from the same PhD programs. Could it be coincidence? Were the local PhD programs a feeder system into the local faculty openings and opportunities? How would I fare in the same intellectual capital marketplace coming from a totally new and non-traditional doctorate program?

A few of the Chicago-land deans I spoke with shined some light on my inquiries. There seemed to be a consensus that a candidate from a new non-traditional doctorate program didn't stand a chance of getting a full-time position at a credible traditional college or university. Furthermore, I was advised that my degree from Argosy University would be assessed by academic elites as worthless. I often heard the following stipulation: "But if you're a good researcher and scholar, you may get some consideration someday."

I did what God told me to do. I believed in myself and the path that I was on. My vision of the future seemed much brighter than I ever imagined. The doctoral level coursework was very challenging and engaging. I had confidence that Argosy's faculty was preparing me to conduct scholarly research and to secure a desired academic position soon.

Eventually, I interviewed and accepted a part-time teaching position at the International Academy of Design and Technology (IADT)-Chicago for the upcoming winter 2003 term. I was very thankful to God for this position. But there were more blessings in store during that season.

I expressed my desire to teach in a traditional university setting to one of my most esteemed mentors, Dr. Robert L. Head. Robert was one of my former professors at Benedictine, and at that time, he was the president of Urbana University. I always admired Robert and held his advice and counsel in the highest regard. He referred me to one of his colleagues. "Cleamon, give Dr. John Eber a call at Saint Xavier University (SXU) and see if he has any opportunities available, be sure to tell him that you know me…"

Have you ever witnessed God work with and through people on your behalf? Surgeons, attorneys, teachers, mentors, and even airline pilots can all serve as a conduit for the will of God to have its perfect way in your life.

The vision of prosperity became clearer as my first day of university teaching drew near. The contents of my written prayer request and covenant had not been forgotten. IADT-Chicago was located downtown. SXU was within a very close driving distance from my home. I felt confident that I would be highly respected and could be a blessing to students at both institutions. Lastly, I believed that if I excelled in the higher education industry, I could realize unlimited earnings.

Chapter 13 – Realizing the vision

Dean Eber called me in for an interview a few days before Christmas in 2002. All the faculty and staff members were gone. We got acquainted and chatted about our common bonds to Robert. He acknowledged my youth in a diplomatic manner. He said, "Wow, you've been busy. You graduated from high school in 1994? I got a kid that graduated in 1992." He offered a positive discussion in regard to my age and background. My ambition and drive were not viewed as suspect.

"Well, I hit the ground running. I began working at GM at age 17, and my parents never allowed me to be a stranger to hard work," I confidently explained. We carried on for the next 15 minutes with light conversation about my previous training and consulting experiences. Then at once, he popped the question, "Are you interested in full-time teaching or part-time?" I was greatly reminded of the age-old cliché "just get your foot in the door." My rebuttal had always been well one foot in the door leaves the "gluteus maximus" outside of the door.

I abandoned the age-old wisdom of clichés and rebuttals and responded, *"Full-time."* He explained that full-time positions had to be budgeted and there is a search committee process that is used to bring in full-time faculty members. However, he assured me that there may be some adjunct (part-time) teaching opportunities available for the summer semester. Our meeting ended very positively. That was the very first but not the last time that I visited SXU's campus.

2003

January marked new beginnings and closure to the wilderness experience. Dean Eber called me during the second week of January to offer me the opportunity to teach two capstone business strategy courses. He said, "The professor who usually teaches these courses has a family emergency and will be taking the semester off; are you interested?" I was surprised by both his call and the offer. I expected something to develop before the summer months, but definitely not before spring. I gleefully responded, "Certainly!"

Teaching at IADT and SXU combined formed a full-time teaching load. The salary of an adjunct professor could easily be 25% or less than that of a full-time professor. I didn't care. Nicole's salary and mine enabled us to get by and meet our financial obligations. She also had a very strong work ethic and commitment to excellence. Nicole encouraged me when I was an engineer to pursue my aspirations of becoming a college professor whenever the opportunity presented itself.

The time had finally come. It was no time to be pragmatic. I had to be the very best professor that I could be. My strategy was simple. Teach at the same level and above the full-time faculty members. Thus, my tactics involved paying great attention to detail, evidencing personal mastery of the subject matter, and establishing a personal rapport with each student. I didn't get into academics to boast about my knowledge and expertise. My primary goal was to prepare students to realize their full potential and to achieve their dreams.

From the very first day of class and forward, I was driven and prepared to prove all of my doubters wrong. The capstone strategy course was challenging to teach. I had to compile and integrate the undergraduate business curriculum into a single course. Was Dean Eber inadvertently using the virtues of the Pygmalion Effect? I didn't know. It did not seem like a head-game. This was real. Students referred to me as "Professor Moorer," because that is who I had become.

Thus, I took command of the subject matter. I did my homework to prepare each lesson plan. Some of my newfound colleagues would stop and stare into my classrooms to see why students were so eager to participate in class discussions and exercises. In this very first semester of college teaching, I began to feel the anointing of the Lord on my skills and my profession.

God gave me the gift to articulate and recall long passages of management theory. There were times that my lectures seemed to be on auto-pilot. It was God and only Him that brought my best to the surface on call.

> *By faith in the name of Jesus, this man whom you see and know was made strong. It is Jesus' name and the faith that comes through him that has given this complete healing to him, as you can all see.*

> — Acts 3:16

The anointing traveled with me between IADT and SXU. I felt God's presence at IADT in both sections of the marketing course that I taught. This realized vision was more than natural; it was ordained.

Several of my students at both institutions asked me, "How old are you and how did you get to this point in life so soon?" I took the time to share with them highlights of my background and my journey. My calling was being realized through my profession. One of my first students adopted me as his life-mentor. Darryl was a very bright and well-spoken young man. "Professor Moorer, you're my guy, and 'the-man', I want to walk in your footsteps," he convincingly stated. Those types of compliments and statements did my heart very well. But I made it a practice not to boast. I dared not to take credit for God's favor in my life.

> *As it is, you boast and brag. All such boasting is evil.*

> — James 4:16

My parents were quite proud of my new career and positions. I had the opportunity of allowing them to sit in on one of my lectures at SXU. It was my father's 75th birthday. He accepted the invitation as if it was a birthday gift. Looking at them in the front row of the classroom was much different from seeing them in the front row during my childhood theatrical performances. This was not an act. I had evolved. But more importantly, times had evolved.

My father shared with me his view of the significance of my journey, path, and evolution. He reminded me of his youth, growing up in the rural south and the limitations and restrictions placed on people of color. He went on to express his happiness by saying, "…and here it is, you are a professor, don't ever drink strong liquor or smoke anything that could harm your mind. I've never seen anyone that sharp and that young talk for an hour and a half about strategy. Best of all, I got a chance to see this in my life time."

My mother was equally joyous. "I never had any doubts, this doesn't surprise me at all," she said. But it surely surprised me. I remembered my journey from being a trouble-maker in grade school to flunking out of college and all the trials that young adulthood brought on.

> *he saved us, not because of righteous things we had done, but because of his mercy. He saved us through the washing of rebirth and renewal by the Holy Spirit,*
>
> — Titus 3:5

Once again, I was excelling at school and work. My doctoral course work had wound down. I was appointed a dissertation chairperson to discuss my dissertation plans and research agenda with. Simultaneously, my deans at both institutions offered me courses to teach for the rest of the year.

I focused my dissertation in the area of change management. My dissertation was titled, "Understanding the significance of employee involvement in planned change efforts." I researched and created a compilation of case studies focused on university planned change processes with a specific focus on university name changes. The topic was multifaceted in that it collectively investigated marketing, OB, and systems thinking. But all of these facets are in the domain of any business environment. I successfully defended my dissertation in the summer of 2004.

I officially became a Doctor of Business Administration. God blessed me to achieve what was once inconceivable. However, this new level of scholastic achievement didn't cement my status as a scholar. I had yet to be granted the opportunity to contend for a tenured faculty position. A candidate must first be on a tenure track to be considered by a university committee for a tenured position.

Tenure-track opportunities are only available in and at traditional colleges or universities. Most tenure-track positions enable a faculty member to teach for a six-year period and then apply for tenure. Tenure in laymen's terms is a *"life-time contract"* to teach at the institution that grants it. Some professors view it as the ultimate form of employment security. As for me, I believe that I have adequately explained that all of my security rests in my faith in God. Where does your feeling of security or protection come from? Is it in your position or the promises of others?

I was teaching twice as many courses as tenured or tenure-track faculty members each semester. In addition, the variety of courses that I was assigned was unparalleled. Marketing, statistics, operations, business, government, and society (BGS), management information systems (MIS), and telecommunications were the courses that I could expect to be assigned in any given term.

By 2005, I was offered and I accepted a full-time non-tenure-track position at SXU. I taught the courses at the locations and in the formats that most of the other faculty members didn't want to teach. I hoped that my diligence would overcome some of the biases that loomed over my doctorate.

This strategy wasn't working. My years of teaching experience were mounting. I applied for internal tenure-track positions, but was never successful in obtaining one.

> *Let us not become weary in doing good, for at the proper time we will reap a harvest if we do not give up.*

> — Galatians 6:9

The administration made me feel like I was good enough to continue to be invited back to teach each year, but I wasn't good enough to contend for a life-time position. It's like being invited out to dinner, but being forewarned not to get full. In lieu of growing bitter, I decided to get better.

I kept a record of each set of end-of-course student evaluation forms from every class that I taught. The overwhelming consensus from many students was, "Dr. Moorer is one of the best, if not the best professor that I've ever had!" These sentiments were expressed by both undergraduate and graduate level students. In addition, I established a research agenda. It became imperative to act as if I was on a tenure track even when I wasn't. I assumed departmental responsibilities and contributed to university-life.

The administrators acknowledged my efforts by continuously asking me to do more work in the same capacity. Most significantly, I was changing students' lives. Students were learning about the discipline, their lives, and the potential of their future through and by my teaching and lectures

The opportunity for promotion and advancement within SXU grew dismal. However, I believed that God would do it for me there or elsewhere. It was more than obvious that I couldn't get on a tenure-track by my own individual merits. But God gave me a dream that reassured me that I was still on the right path, and that I was on my way to promise.

One night, I dreamt that I was walking along a path filled with coins on the ground. Initially, I would sneak to pick up the coins and put them in my pocket without anyone seeing me. As I walked forward and into the light that God provided, the coins became more plentiful. But the coins wouldn't continue to appear, unless I continued to walk forward. When I stopped walking, the coins disappeared. I began to run, praise, and dance in my dream, and the coins rained down plentifully.

I concluded from the dream that all that I received and would receive would continue to come from God. My work at SXU was for *Him* and not for those who were opposing me. My job was to continue to believe and to continue to faithfully walk along the path that God set for me.

By myself I can do nothing; I judge only as I hear, and my judgment is just, for I seek not to please myself but him who sent me.

– John 5:30

Chapter 14 – A Bittersweet

2007

I spoke to every key administrator regarding my desire to obtain a tenure-track position. Each administrator seemed to speak in riddles. None of them could directly articulate a concern or issue that disqualified me from it. It was a game of diversion, as each stakeholder group was benefiting greatly by my continued service.

> *This calls for patient endurance on the part of the saints who obey God's commandments and remain faithful to Jesus.*
>
> — Revelations 14:12

To my surprise, one of the institution's most distinguished administrators commented, "It doesn't matter how long it takes to get on a tenure track, or how long it takes to get tenure as long as you get it." This truly didn't make any sense. In many institutions, incoming faculty members negotiate to waive some of the required years of the tenure track. Likewise, many institutions allow this provision in their bylaws to attract and retain experienced faculty.

> *Do your best to present yourself to God as one approved, a workman who does not need to be ashamed and who correctly handles the word of truth.*
>
> — 2 Timothy 2:15

It became imperative for me to explore external options and to continue to refine my transferable competencies, if I had to move on to another institution. I began teaching online courses at Walden University. The distance learning model enabled me to increase my span of influence across the entire world. Over the last several years, I have had the honor of meeting and teaching students from every continent, except Antarctica.

As my competencies continued to increase, my determination to get onto a tenure track also heightened. The subtle excuse that most of the administrators uttered referred to their scrutiny of my DBA. For the record, Argosy University was accredited by the same regional body that accredited all of the traditional colleges and universities in our region. In addition, my first peer-reviewed journal article publication was another testament to the efficacy of my scholastic training.

> *The LORD will make you the head, not the tail. If you pay attention to the commands of the LORD your God that I give you this day and carefully follow them, you will always be at the top, never at the bottom.*

> – Deuteronomy 28:13

My father always told me that life's greatest triumphs are often a result of your ability to travel through the bitterness of the wilderness to get to the sweetness of the sunshine. I didn't foresee that I would soon be dealing with him in that same light.

In February of 2007, I had a dream that my father passed away. I'd had dreams in the past of things to come. However, in the realms of selective retention and perceptual defense, it is often natural to embrace the pleasant dreams as premonitions. And of course, many of us label unpleasant dreams as nightmares. My tears and the sorrows of that dream awoke me from my sleep. I talked it over with Nicole and we both decided not to worry.

He had just celebrated his 79th birthday and seemed to be very healthy. However, there was the issue of dementia that caused him to be confused and to experience short-term memory loss. I was able to ignore the validity and implication of my dream until Father's Day weekend.

My mother called us over to tell us that Dad was not feeling well. She wondered if she should take him to the hospital. I asked him, "Dad what's going on, how do you feel?" In a faint voice he replied, "I'm tired through and through."

The emergency room doctors immediately placed him into the intensive care unit (ICU). He had suffered from a heart attack and his heart was operating at 15% of its capacity. Life had never prepared me for the days and weeks ahead.

I knew that I had to be strong for my mother. She sat with him in the ICU, both day and night for the first couple of days that he was there. I visited him during the day every day of the first week. He awoke from a nap and had a message for me. "Son, I need you to put one of my cars in your garage, if you have room, because I'll be going away in a few days." I fought back the tears and racing emotions to rub his head and console him as he went back to sleep.

I selfishly thought, "…how could God be taking away my Daddy?" How will my mother go on? When and how will he pass? Sure, I prayed for his recovery. But I could not ignore his age, his condition, and the prior dream that I had pertaining to this season. My biggest surprise and his greatest lesson for me were still yet to come.

By the end of the week following his admission into the hospital, his spirits were really high. Nicole and I visited him and my mother in the ICU. This visit was like none other. He was singing every gospel hymn under the sun. His singing was coupled with tears and laughter. I asked, "Dad why are you crying?" He replied, "…because I'm happy. God told me to get ready and stay ready… and that's what I am going to do."

He continued to entertain us during the visit by joking and telling the story of how and where he met my mother. Dad also reassured me that I hit the jackpot when I met Nicole. I'll never forget how this dying man carried on in the ICU.

My father touched my heart by telling me how he really felt about me. Following one of his solos he said, "Son, I'll never forget what you did for us. I was down and out in Detroit and didn't see my way out. You came and moved us up here. I love you and I'll never be able to repay you. Whatever

I have it is yours. If you need a few bucks or see that you are in jam, don't hesitate to ask old Dad. I'll give you whatever I have. By the way, you are glowing. You look like such a Godly Man, son."

He didn't allow us to openly pity him. It was obvious that God was with him, and that *He* was coming to get him. He had his mind made up and his heart and soul fixed on God. I never imagined that my father would teach me both how to live and how to die. After seven weeks of toiling with his condition, he ascended into Heaven to be with God on August 8, 2007.

> *What does the worker gain from his toil? I have seen the burden God has laid on men. He has made everything beautiful in its time. He has also set eternity in the hearts of men; yet they cannot fathom what God has done from beginning to end. I know that there is nothing better for men than to be happy and do good while they live.*
>
> — Ecclesiastes 3:9-12

How was I to move on? One day at a time was the approach that I chose to cope with his death. I had to try to be happy by knowing that God made him whole by taking him home. The days and weeks after his death were filled with tears and longing to see his smile and hear his voice. I directed my sorrow to fighting for my rightful position in academia. Secondly, I urgently began to diagnose and reexamine my purpose and life plan.

The game of charades at SXU had grown old and dull. I spoke candidly to the new dean of the business school about my contributions and tenure-track aspiration. "Everything but the Argosy degree looks good. I'm looking for candidates from top business programs for our accreditation pursuits. Non-traditional programs just won't work," he exclaimed. I was familiar with the accreditation guidelines and stipulations. I had memorized the academic and professional requirements for each faculty member. "The qualifying document doesn't say that a candidate from a non-traditional PhD program is not academically qualified," I boldly stated.

I further explained that many B-schools with the accreditation that we aspire to earn determine academic qualification on the number of scholastic contributions and the doctorate. "So do two scholastic publications in a five-year period make me academically-qualified," I asked. "I don't know how many it will take for you to be academically qualified," he cynically remarked.

Okay, so they didn't want me there. How do you handle bias and partiality? Take the time to pray for those who deter you from your goals. Don't give up! Do know that God has something much better in store for you.

> *I will give you the treasures of darkness, riches stored in secret places, so that you may know that I am the LORD, the God of Israel, who summons you by name.*
>
> — Isaiah 45:3

I had come much too far. There was entirely too much at stake. There was no way that I would leave the profession that God blessed me to excel in. My life had become a testimony. I diligently assumed the responsibility and obligation of inspiring, motivating, and teaching thousands of young minds. Promise soon awaited me and nothing could stop me from receiving and embracing it.

A colleague told me about an opening at Trinity Christian College. I decided to visit the campus and to apply for the tenure-track business management faculty position. The provost was pleased to make me an offer within one week of my interview. It was amazing that Trinity Christian College was able make a determination in three weeks that SXU had failed to make in five and a half years.

> *The end of a matter is better than its beginning, and patience is better than pride.*
>
> — Ecclesiastes 7:8

I still had one academic year to complete at SXU. In the second month of the first semester, I received a letter from the dean to notify me that my contract wouldn't be renewed for the upcoming school year. Some of my mentors suggested that I buy my time wisely. Thus, I only focused on teaching my classes. I removed myself from all boards and committees. I was able to focus on my research agenda and to reflect on Dad's transition in my newfound spare time. In my most earnest attempt to be withdrawn from departmental activities, destiny still had to prevail.

A few years earlier, the university formed a diversity committee to examine the cultural and social inner workings of the institution. Each department and business unit had to form its own subcommittee. I believe that I was selected to serve on our department's committee for some rather obvious reasons. The leader of the committee invited me to the meeting to discuss the department's diversity plan, goals, and outcomes.

The meeting commenced as if I wasn't sitting in the room for the first 15 minutes. "I know we're doing a good job with diversity, most of our last applicants were very ethnically diverse," said the leader. "Yes, maybe we could be a model for the rest of the university, because we are doing such a fine job with our diversity efforts," one member added. The conversation continued about ways to advertise in ethnically diverse publications and the prospect of joining minority-oriented professional organizations.

I didn't understand how a room full of professionals could only view diversity from the lens of racial/ethnic diversification. What about the factors of socio-economic, political, physical (abilities), age, gender, psychographics, and sexual orientation? It was clear that the meeting was a formality. I couldn't take it any longer.

I interjected by saying, "How about we engage in an authentic discussion about diversity by asking diverse individuals about their experiences in this institution?" One of my dearest colleagues at the time responded by asking, "Clem, is there something on your mind?" That was all that I needed to get started. "As a matter of fact, there is…"

I related the entire experience of my negative attempts to secure a tenure-track position within the university. Most of the members present were very familiar with my plight. I explained that bias and partiality based on misinterpreted standards is unacceptable and counterproductive to the true pursuit of diversity. The committee's leader furiously responded by saying, "…the standards are not biased on the basis of age and race." My issue pertained to the misapplication and misinterpretation of the standards. I reminded him of our conversation at the beginning of the school year. I boldly declared, "Anytime you insert your own beliefs and biases into an accrediting body's standards you are potentially breaching trust and integrity." With no shame, he replied, "Those aren't just my biases, they are shared biases."

We were finally getting somewhere. He had admitted that he used shared biases as a sufficient means to disqualify me. He augmented the standards to match his own intended desires. Why did this meeting and fight matter so much to me? I had attained a new job several months prior. The argument was for those coming behind me. I didn't plan for any of that to come out during the meeting.

However, it really felt good. I continued to draw on greater points regarding the correlation between academic affiliation and aptitude. I offered the well-known example of Bill Gates dropping out of Harvard to start Microsoft. Then I asked, "What about Benjamin Banneker, who taught himself astronomy and created a clock that kept perfect time for 50 years, independent of formal education?"

Countless numbers of individuals have soared and achieved great heights independent of a particular college or university's affiliation. I added that perhaps there is positive correlation between academic affiliation and aptitude, but academic affiliation isn't and shouldn't ever be considered the only and most important variable.

Basically, God provided an opportunity for me to tell them that my departure was indeed their loss. Not only was I good enough for the position, I was too good to continue to be treated as though I was inferior. In the faintest voice, I could hear Dad cheer, "You tell them Son; now that's how you cook his goose!"

I caution that speaking up against injustice shouldn't be about getting people told. The intended outcomes of confrontation should be a mutual better understanding, respect for differences, and an appreciation for idea-sharing and exchange. Even though it felt good, I repented to God, just in case my bold proclamations of truth proved harmful to others.

You prepare a table before me in the presence of my enemies. You anoint my head with oil; my cup overflows. Surely goodness and love will follow me all the days of my life, and I will dwell in the house of the LORD forever.

– Psalm 23:5-6

Chapter 15 – Just the Beginning

The transition from SXU to Trinity Christian College was very peaceful. Both institutions were equipped with scholars and intellectuals. Many of Trinity's scholars were very well versed in biblical and interdisciplinary subjects. I enjoyed debates and discussion with some of the faculty regarding the merit and potential virtue of ethical business practices.

I spent most of my time in between classes delving into my research agenda. The cross-sections of OB, strategy, and international business intrigued me. Most Christian colleges and universities offer a unique opportunity for meditation, reflection, and exploration.

The work-life of many tenured and tenure-track professors is of little burden and stress, as compared to other professions. I could easily envision getting self-consumed by my success. The way of the world fosters or perpetuates not only self-gloating but self-indulgence. But the uncommon path and nature of my ascension to the rank of professor wouldn't allow me to become self-centric or contemptuous.

> *When you enter the land the LORD your God is giving you, do not learn to imitate the detestable ways of the nations there.*
>
> – Deuteronomy 18:9

Before leaving SXU, I had begun to focus on the topic of corporate social responsibility (CSR).

My mind and my heart both longed to understand how social justice, peace, and harmony could be achieved through international business. I've always detested the crimes derived from corporate greed coupled by the great economic and social disparities of nations.

The Spirit of God directed my attention to the world's poorest regions. I began to understand that I've been equipped all of these years to seek and devise means to use global business and international commerce to reduce and eradicate some of the world's greatest social ills.

I am disturbed by poverty and genocide. Aren't you also outraged by the horrible circumstances that millions of global citizens come to know as the status quo? I started my life pursuits and journey with hope. It is unacceptable for me to take a deaf ear and a blind eye to the world's poor, sick and diseased.

Just when I thought that I evolved into the scholar and professional that I always wanted to be, I realized that this juncture was truly the beginning. Doctors are called and anointed to fix and repair human systems. The human systems that permit human trafficking, genocide, and child prostitution have an indescribable need for modification and recalibration.

I challenged myself to believe that it didn't matter how brilliant or highly esteemed I'd become, if I don't make the world better for those who can't do it for themselves. My research leaped from the pragmatic discussions of business curriculum development and change management to global CSR to cooperatively eradicate genocide and to reduce poverty.

Indeed, I am suggesting that leaders of global corporations, national and foreign governments, the United Nations, clergy, scholars, and global citizens should unite to bring an end to genocide in Darfur and in other regions.

Economic gain and prosperity have always been some of the root causes of dehumanization and deprivation. My role models and mentors were no longer the sitcom, "A Different World's", main character, 'Dwayne Wayne' and my High School buddy Amos. I began to desire to emulate the selfless works of Ghandi, Dr. Martin Luther King, Jr., and

Mother Theresa. They all overcame great personal struggles and battles to bring healing to nations.

Had my walk and journey prepared me to begin a new path as a global change agent? How do we ensure that children in every nation have a sense of hope for better days? I encourage you to use your talents, energies, and resources to help the helpless. I am a firm believer in the power of philanthropy. Giving without intimidation and recompense is Godly.

> *I tell you the truth, anyone who has faith in me will do what I have been doing. He will do even greater things than these, because I am going to the Father.*
>
> *– John 14:12*

God has also taught us the importance of wisdom and understanding. I researched the linkages between wealthy nations and natural resources such as diamonds, gold, and petroleum. The common thread of the world's wealthiest nations is their ability to trade, share, and barter resources. Likewise, the most common thread of the world's poorest nations is either their citizens' lack of access to and control of resources or the nation's inability to demand trade and commercial investments from other nations.

During my second semester at Trinity, I traveled to Taipei, Taiwan to examine international trade first-hand and to get a better understanding of the Island's relationships with some of the world's poorest and wealthiest nations. I met Christian business leaders who shared some of my concerns and ideas about global CSR and the world's greatest social ills. We discussed how the biotechnological, semiconductor, and furniture industries could tentatively work to ensure that ethical operations are the only mode of business within their enterprises.

My hopes began to grow as I constructed mental models of global CSR and their potential efficacies. It isn't enough to divest from nations that employ inhumane practices and that perpetuate genocide. The Sudan Accountability and Divestment Act is a step in the right direction. But many of our world's wealthiest and most powerful companies and countries are not taking the same measures to disable genocidal activities.

I returned from overseas with an unquenchable desire to get involved in global peace efforts. Great professors are often driven to academic institutions that are in alignment and in full support of their scholastic intentions and endeavors. Trinity was a fine institution, very collegial, and committed to the intellectual and spiritual development of its students.

However, I needed to be at an institution that fully understood my passion and calling to travel, conduct research, and energize students to take the challenge of changing the world. I frequently taught courses at Roosevelt University in Chicago. Roosevelt University's president was committed to perpetuating the theme of social justice. My passion and calling had extended and grown far beyond the discussion of social justice to a much broader global citizenship and world peace initiative.

Upon returning to the US, I promised to give a guest-lecture in one of my most distinguished colleagues' classes at Dominican University. Dr. Al Rosenbloom and I met while we were both teaching at SXU. He is both a good friend and a scholar in every sense of the terms. Al shared with me many of Dominican University's Brennan School of Business's (BSB) programming goals and efforts in their Center for Peace through Global Commerce.

I had applied for a tenure-track position at Dominican University before I began my university teaching career. When I initially visited the campus to apply in 2002, I didn't want to leave it. The university's architecture, ambiance, and learning environment indescribably appealed to me. But I wasn't ready back in 2002. God knew that I wasn't ready then. I had no idea that God was preparing me for this season of promise all along.

> *However, as it is written: "No eye has seen, no ear has heard, no*
> *mind has conceived what God has prepared for those who love him"*
> — 1 Corinthians 2:9

The dean of the BSB, Dr. Arvid Johnson, sat in Dr. Rosenbloom's class during my guest-lecture. Dean Arvid Johnson admired my teaching style and competence. He offered me an opportunity to join the BSB faculty on a part-time basis. I accepted with an understanding that if and when a full-time position became available I should feel encouraged to apply for it.

I competed for the position with candidates from some of the most prestigious universities in the world. God showed me that it didn't matter, whether I went to Oxford, Stanford, Harvard, Northwestern, MIT, or Yale; what he had for me was for me.

At age 33, I sat in my new office as a full-time Assistant Professor of Management in Dominican University's BSB. My heart was more than overjoyed by the opportunity to have shared this story with you. I had dreams along the way of having course-work that I never completed. Those particular dreams have discontinued. I've completed the course by sharing and telling you the story of how and what God did for me.

I saw myself being promoted to the rank of Associate Professor and being tenured several years down the road. Most importantly, I had plans to go to seminary and to start a global not-for-profit organization called the Humanity Agenda (HA). The HA's sole intent will be to cooperatively engage global corporations in the eradication of genocide and the reduction of poverty. I ultimately desire to help children around the world realize hope and promise. Our greatest failure would be not to spread the gospel of Jesus Christ and to forgo the responsibility of making this world better than how we found it.

Yes, you will get to the top! Indeed, you can become more than you ever thought that you would be able to. You can go as far as your faith will take you. God does want you to be in a position of power and authority. He wants to bless you so that you can be a blessing to others. You may not experience all that I've gone through to achieve great promise. In fact, you may or will experience even greater challenges and circumstances on your way to promise. I pray that you have envisioned your destiny of promise and favor by reading my story. Thank you for allowing me to share this miraculous testament to God's power and unlimited ability with you. In closing, please remember the words of Winston Churchill: *"Never give in. Never give in. Never, never, never, never -- in nothing, great or small, large or petty -- never give in, except to convictions of honour and good sense. Never yield to force. Never yield to the apparently overwhelming might of the enemy."*

Backtrack – "The Epilogue"

Many authors of biographical memoirs decide to provide their readers with an epilogue to describe some of the major developments and events that transpired after the release of their original work. Initially, I didn't plan to offer a new release after such a short period of time. But various circumstances and a timely recurring epiphany urged me to do so. The sections of the original memoir: On Track, Off Track, New Track, Fast Track, and Tenure Track are incomplete without this epilogue section, properly dubbed, Backtrack. Backtrack is intended to further encourage and inspire you to dream and to work to achieve goals that improve the lives of others as you reach your full potential and promise. This section will not serve as a summation of From Failure to Promise: An Uncommon Path to Professoriate, but it will provide a 360-Degree snapshot of my original journey with a refreshingly, climatic finish and a clear "call to action".

2010 – The Making of From Failure to Promise

I toiled with the idea and concept of the book for close to a decade. Yes, in 2002, when Nicole and I were struggling to make a go of our management consulting firm, (Moorer Customer Care Solutions Consulting), the thought of writing a memoir occupied my mind during some of my idle moments. At that time, I didn't feel like I had enough substance to compose a piece of timeless literature. Sure, I had become an engineer, global service executive, and independent consultant following my comeback from academic failure, but I knew there was much more to achieve.

At the beginning of 2010, I was completely compelled to share with the world how God transformed me from being a college flunk-out to a university professor. I no longer believed that I had a choice in the matter. I began to evaluate my journey and came to the conclusion that if I were to create a legacy, that was the time to do so. As you've probably noted from reading this book, at times I digress to elaborate on a teachable moment, or I take the opportunity to provide some anecdotal context to support the ideas or stories that I am describing. I apologize to the readers who are slightly distracted by this writing style. I subscribe to one of the rules of writing provided by the late Mr. Elmore Leonard, "If it sounds like writing, I rewrite it." One of my main goals pertaining to writing From Failure to Promise was to be able to have an interesting conversation with readers through the use of a relatable narrative that encouraged self-reflection and introspection. You are reading this book for your own personal reasons. So I chose to write it with you: the reader, in mind.

Now back to the discussion of legacy, how can this memoir serve as a key construct of my legacy? Secondly, how could the legacy of a complete stranger affect you? I am using legacy in the connotative sense of transcending something of value to others. I've meditated on the concept of my personal legacy and concluded that if I am able to impact, influence, and inspire others positively then I have indeed created a legacy. Even further, if my positive impact, influence, or inspiration on readers encourages them to improve the lives of others, then I will be even more thrilled and fulfilled.

Consider all of your past and present heroes. I am confident that they have provided you with some type of positive impact, influence, or inspiration. I became a huge fan of Dr. Ben Carson when I was 19 years-old. I read his book, "Think Big", at a very pivotal point in my life. I was not only in awe about the fact that he evolved from very humble beginnings to become one of the world's greatest pediatric neurosurgeons, but I was also amazed at how he was willing to share and encourage others to achieve greatness. Dr. Ben Carson, Booker T. Washington, Mahatma Ghandi, Dr. Maya Angelou, and Dr. Myles Munroe are a handful of authors who impacted, influenced, and inspired me to write From Failure to Promise.

I began writing From Failure to Promise: An Uncommon Path to Professoriate on February 1, 2010. I wrote for 140 consecutive days so that I could complete the first draft of the manuscript by Father's Day. I chose to fast between the hours of midnight and 3:00PM each day and I limited my beverage consumption to lemon water during that span of time. I wanted to be able to think, reflect, and write clearly with divine inspiration. Creating the chapter titles, chapter outlines, and selecting which stories and scriptural references to share in each chapter was the first and perhaps most important step in my development of the memoir.

In the midst of my writing, on April 30, 2010, Nicole gave me the look that I had only seen three more than memorable times before. It was time to drop everything and head to the hospital for the birth of our fourth child, Colomon Levi Moorer. Fortunately, Colomon was born healthy, whole, and happy. He unlike his brothers was a quiet baby, who actually went to sleep at night for the first several months of his life. His maturity and selflessness, if you will, helped to enable me to complete the first draft of From Failure to Promise by mid-June. I reserved most of the month of July for rewriting, editing, and proof-reading.

As for publishing and distribution, I chose to pursue the self-publishing and distribution route. I am extremely pleased that I had taken that approach. The self-publishing option gave me the autonomy and freedom to choose what, when, where, and how to connect with you. In addition, you the reader and the marketplace were able to clearly assess and express how you felt about From Failure to Promise: An Uncommon Path to Professoriate. Readers' feedback made the original memoir #1 in the genre of Biographies/Memoirs by Educators on Amazon.

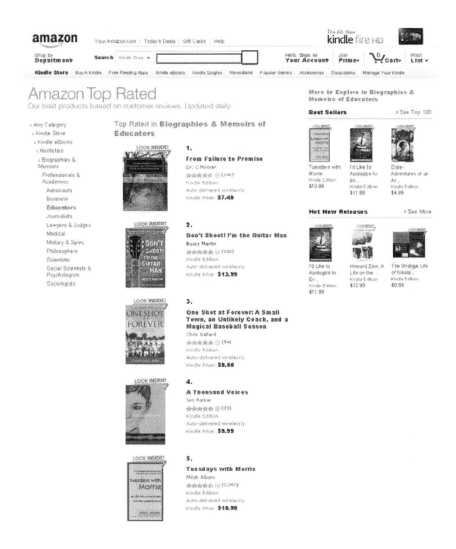

My successful publication of From Failure to Promise: An Uncommon Path to Professoriate was tremendously marred and forced to take a backseat to an act of God that I feared and deeply dreaded, but I was clearly forewarned of.

Dorris Jean Moorer

Over the years, I grew to realize that many of the lessons that we learn in life have a way of repeating themselves at seemingly some of the most inopportune times. Shortly after Colomon was born, I had a dream that my mother was going to pass away soon. I used the same proximity between the dream pertaining to my father's passing and his actual transition as a prediction of sorts for the foreseen departure of Mom. Six months wasn't enough time to say goodbye. But in comparison to the sudden and tragic instances of losing a loved one without any type of forewarning, six months is certainly more time to accept and to prepare for the grief caused by losing a loved one. In hindsight, I did have more than six months to prepare. Just a few years earlier, she had also been diagnosed with congestive heart failure and an autoimmune disease, (Sjogren's Syndrome). Sjogren's had progressively taken a greater toll on her both physically and mentally.

As many of you have or will experience when your loved one suffers you suffer also. The scent of the long hospital halls and corridors had become more than familiar to me; for several years they'd become a part of me to an extent. Do know that you and other visitors are your hospitalized friend or loved one's source of strength. Even when or if they ask you, "*How do I look?*"…"*Are you worried about me?*" Please try to continue to provide them with hope. I can provide this advice because I lived through these scenarios on more than the few occasions described in this memoir.

Mom had begun to exist as a shell of her former self and her health sharply declined during the month of August. I went to visit her in the hospital on Sunday, August 15, 2010. Had I known it would be the last time that I would see Mother alive, would I have done or said anything differently? I really don't think so. She called me when I was on my way to the hospital and asked me if I would bring her a slice of yellow cake with chocolate icing from the local bakery. Being the good son, that I strived to be, I brought her two of the largest slices available. We laughed and talked for hours. She asked me more about From Failure to Promise and probed me about my decision to dedicate it to my father.

She playfully suggested that I loved my dad more than I loved her. I promised her that something great would come along someday, and that I would take the opportunity to dedicate something really special and significant to her. I too wanted the entire world to know how great of a mother she was and the invaluable impact her faith and nourishment had on me.

So we shifted from that conversation…"about who do you love the most", to highlight some of the other very memorable moments during my upbringing and early adulthood. She acknowledged that Nicole was the daughter that she never had and that I better continue to be good to her. We also discussed my relationship with my brother, Julian, which had improved greatly over the last few years. Seeing him and his children (Jasmine and Terrance) during the Mother's Day weekend of 2010 was certainly a timely, and much cherished recollection for her. She continuously acknowledged that she was proud of both of her sons and her six grandchildren. As her nurses came in and out of her room, she never hesitated to reintroduce me to them and remind them that her son is a "Doctor". Our time together was sweet, organic, and divine, apparently by God's design.

I stayed at least two hours past the visiting hour of 8:00PM. *"Do you know how proud I am of you?"*, she asked. Her verbal strokes and compliments were coupled with instructions and even more inquiries. As I explicitly recall, she made the following statements to me: *"No matter what, I want you to keep going ,and go all the way to the top"… "Are you disappointed that you and Nicole didn't have a little girl? What are you going to do with four boys?"* I could only smile and rub my Mother's hand during this conversation, because I could tell that some of her medications were causing her to ramble a bit. I knew what the "no matter what…" meant, in theory, but I still didn't want to apply it.

A few days had gone by, and Nicole and I were preparing to get Cleamon III ready for the new school year. I didn't know that Mother's Passing was literally upon us. But on August 18th, while I was driving to work, the 1973 hit song, *"I'll always love my Mama…she brought me in this world…"* by The Intruders, came on the radio, it gave me a strange feeling.

I immediately called Mom and she explained that she was feeling very rough. But she guaranteed me that she had been praying and talking to Jesus continuously over the last several hours. Mom further reiterated that she knew that God heard her and all of her business with Him was in order. I planned to visit her in the hospital that day, but it was too late in the evening when I returned home. Coincidentally the first copy of From Failure to Promise arrived in the mail that day and I was going to deliver it to her, but unfortunately, I never got the opportunity to do so.

The phone rang At 2:10AM on Thursday, August 19th. I thought it was my mom returning my call, because I had put in a call to her earlier that night. "Hello, is this Cleamon?" the man on the other end asked. I exclaimed that it was me…he went on to ask if I were driving or alone at the time. My heart began to skip beats in the worst way as I hung on to each word that proceeded from his mouth.

"I am Dr. _____ . Your mother went into cardiac arrest tonight, we rushed her to the ICU, and we were able to revive her initially…. but our 2nd attempt was unsuccessful. She passed away, but it was peaceful; she didn't suffer or struggle. I am sorry for your loss."

I was a total wreck. I headed toward a downward spiral in the days and months ahead. Handling Mother's final arrangements, communicating with Julian and her siblings; and lastly cleaning and removing all of her belongings from her apartment challenged every single fiber of my being. Of course I prayed for strength, fortitude, and understanding. The pain and anguish cut so deeply that I tried to find comfort in a more than occasional, alcoholic beverage. Dad had forewarned me years ago about the dangers of alcohol consumption. Word of advice… if you have a problem that you would like to make larger, then pour some alcohol on it. That single problem can spread into a myriad of greater problems and issues. Another problem that emerges from seeking peace by way of alcohol consumption is a clear inability to realize that life doesn't stop for mourning and mourning doesn't stop for life. Mourning and living coexist, and time seems to be one of the only proven, relief agents, not alcohol.

Could I drink my way out of sorrow? If for any reason that particular question seemed rhetorical in my mind, my loved ones and true friends provided adamant and admonishing rebuttals to my divergent, but temporal muse. It goes without saying that Nicole understood my state of mind, but she wasn't the least bit amused by my new liquid, *jolly-horses*, if you will. I am so thankful that she had not been working alone to keep me on track.

My great friend, Mr. Patrick Franklin, whom I've known since my days at the telephone company, helped me to move from out of this personal abyss. He would strongly suggest in a more than concerned manner that I stay strong, and in his own words, "…Clem, you can't start hitting the hard liquor on a regular." I knew his connotation of "regular" meant frequent or regular basis. Your true friends will tell you the truth and insist that you avoid harmful habits or behaviors at all costs. I didn't have to fight this bout alone; and for that, I will always be eternally grateful. Nicole, Patrick, Diane, Rodney, John, Al and other very close friends would not let me fall.

Patrick stayed in my ear and reminded me that greater days were ahead. Not only was Patrick there to help me emotionally, but he also physically helped me to remove all of my parents' belongings out of their home. He fended off the would-be claimers of unmarked boxes and possessions as we devised our work plan for each day of that grueling task. We got all of the moving and cleaning done within two days. It was one of the most difficult things that I ever imagined having to do. Much of the grief that I experienced came as I uncovered so many of my parents' personal artifacts.

For instance, when you're a six-year old and you make your mother, father, aunt, uncle, or grandparent a keepsake with the assistance of your 1st grade teacher, it could very well be the proudest moment of your existence. Hopefully your pride is substantiated by the gleeful reception and the words that the recipient gives you upon acceptance of this invaluable treasure, right? When we use the term "forever" with children, they seem to interpret it as an earthly infinity of sorts. "I'm going to keep this forever!" Even as a mature adult, you can find yourself hit with the reality that an earthly forever in the sense of the term is an impossibility. So what did I give my parents that they were able to move forward with?

I asked myself. Obviously, it wasn't the house that I bought them, gifts, or the artifacts that I handcrafted during my grade school days. I firmly believe that the love, respect, and honor I showed them when they were living may've made it a little easier for them to close their eyes for the last time, at the end of their earthly days.

I would be remiss if I didn't share with you two letters that I found written by Mother. These letters were prayers to God. Each of these letters served as timely inflection points to help me to better understand the assignment that God gave me in regards to my parents.

Dear Lord, Thank you for my life, my husband, my sons, mother, sisters, and brothers. We need help Jesus. First forgive me Lord, for every wrong deed or thought, whether I knew, or if I did not know. Father, I stretch my hands to thee, no other help I know. Please have mercy on us. We need healing Lord, my husband and I both are ill. We are in a predicament where he still needs to work for a living. We are over-loaded in debt. It is overwhel-ming for I and he. Father, in the name of Jesus, your son, please bring us a way out of all of this debt. Since my husband has been ill, we have borrowed from credit cards, family and acquaintances. Help us to pay these people back, and main-

tain our obligations. I'm looking for a Miracle, because the
sky is the limit to what I can
have. You have all the money
and assets I need. I get emotional and feel down under,
when I ask my family for
money. I know that you know
all about all our problems.
Bless all those that have helped
us, and showed any concern.
Take care of children, and please
help them. We thank you for
everything you have already
done. Our integrity is being
challenged. Send someone that
will work at the shop. Give
my husband the strength and
willpower to work, as he desires.
Take care of us Jesus, and please
hear our prayers. We will be
careful to give you the praise

(over)

for our deliverance! We know you can and above all, We know you will. We Love you, Lord and will forever praise you. Thank you Jesus! If I had ten thousand tongues, it would not be enough to thank you.

Upon reading this particular letter, I realized that I was the answer to my parent's prayer in 2000. It was truly time for them to retire and to close the doors of C&M Collision. God used me and Nicole as vessels to help them to get up and out a very perilous situation. How much sorrow was I supposed to feel? I learned that grief alone could be extremely traumatizing. But I am thankful that my grief was not coupled with guilt.

Self-pity and wallowing in sorrow in review of this particular letter didn't make any sense to me. I had to get up off the floor once again and shift my mental paradigms. I had to turn grief into gratefulness, pity into purpose, mourning into motivation, and sorrow into strength. My new mindset was most helpful for enabling me to accept my mother's last letter to God.

Oh Lord have mercy. The aches, pains, sores, fatigue, Lord, I feel pick, and I truly need you. Please help me to carry on. It's getting a bit ruff, but you promised to never leave me. Thank you Jesus, Please help me. Lord have mercy on me. I love Jesus, yes I do. I believe you will hear my prayer. Thank you Lord.

I still cry a bit when I read my mom's last letter to God. I imagine that Mom wrote this letter during the last week of her life. The illness that she prayed about in 2000, had multiplied into several other ailments. God himself did have mercy on her, and He brought her home to be with Him, forever and ever. My understanding of "forever and everlasting" life was then crystalized.

> *For God so loved the world that he gave his one and only Son, that whoever believes in him shall not perish but have eternal life.*

>   -- John 3:16

It is more than obvious to me that Mom and Dad believed and are now enjoying their eternal lives with God. I closed out 2010 with the reality that 2011 would be the first year that I'd be without my mother's presence.

What about the millions of young children around the world who no longer have living parents? They are forced to go through life without any of the (biological) parental support and love that I received from my parents for over 30 years. Many of these children and young adults' stories don't start out like Chapter One of this memoir: "It began with hope". Their memoirs may begin with the notion that, "It began hopelessly". With the ever present reality of this recurring epiphany in regards to the amount of widespread hopelessness, I realized that the From Failure to Promise platform had to be broadened to equip, energize, encourage, and empower readers to transform the lives of others, even by merely prompting local and global citizens to be mindful and dutiful in their roles of creating a better world.

2011 - Renewed Purpose – (Scholarships and Educators' Grants)

In early 2011, I discovered that From Failure to Promise had to be much more than a book, it needed to serve as a catalyst to a movement. I wanted the message of From Failure to Promise to find its intended audience, and also to capture its audience in a most compelling manner. I am sure that most authors are hopeful that their work reaches the masses, or their projected target of the mass population. I had to redefine "*reach*" for my own purposes. Many marketers use the term reach to identify the performance of a specific set of marketing efforts.

I grew to not be as concerned about how many copies of From Failure to Promise actually sold. I became absorbed in the direct feedback that I received from readers. Several readers contacted me to express how the book inspired and commissioned them to act positively on the behalf of others. I couldn't quantify the value of positively impacting one single person in a positive manner. There are thousands of books in print that have sold millions of copies, but have had no real transformative impact on readers. I would prefer to sell one copy of From Failure to Promise that positively impacts one person rather than to sell millions of copies that inspire no reflection, hope, or positive action.

I began to think more and more about my journey and revisited the fact that I needed most of the insights and lessons presented in the book during the transformative years of my life. Most people who are committed to continuous growth and change will find that transformation is a life-long process. I firmly believe in the concept of life-long learning. Thus, the "student audience" became the intended target of From Failure to Promise. I use the term, "student" very loosely. I am referring to "students of life", in a general sense. Which may indeed, be everyone.

This is a very diverse target and population. I am still and will always be a student too. I study, investigate, and think deeply about matters pertaining to the human condition. Even as an academic, I often encourage my students to apply business concepts, theories, and applications to healing or solving some of society's greatest woes. I pondered whether my role as an author of a personal memoir had to be any different than my role as an academic. I concluded that my roles as an academic, change agent, and good global citizen would only be further validated by my ability to connect with an audience or community of readers far outside the confines of my lecture hall. This realization led us to develop the From Failure to Promise Scholarship and Educator's Grant Fund. We wanted to add more layers to our commitment to altruism. It was not enough for me to stop at only wanting readers to excel and to reach their full promise. We responded to the unrelenting gut-level urge to try to develop ways to fund and close the financial gap for students and educators in order to better help them to reach their full potential.

While we were in the process of laying the groundwork for what would later become Dr. C Moorer & Associates, Inc., my success as a tenure-track professor was continuing to heighten. Please allow me to add a quick, anecdotal insertion to this section. When you decide to address the needs of others you do not have to be overly consumed with how you are going to fulfill your own needs.

God is not unjust; he will not forget your work and the love you have shown him as you have helped his people and continue to help th----

- Hebrews 6:10

I fully understand that in many societies taking care of one's self is a top priority. You may even ask or have asked yourself: "…how am I going to help someone else when I need help myself?" Good question. I have learned that at times life can be a piecemeal of sorts. While you are working to build the best possible life that you can for yourself and family, there are others near or around you that could use some of your experience or knowledge to improve their own lives. None of us will ever just have it all together in our personal, professional, or spiritual lives. There will always be room for improvement.

So as I was seeking new ways to improve my teaching and research, I received a tap that I could only dream of. One of my former students reached out to me to tell me about a vacancy and active search for a Dean of the School of Business position at another institution that was very similar to Dominican University. She was an employee there and she shared with me that she believed that I would be a good candidate for the Deanship position.

I wasn't actively pursuing or even thinking about the role of dean. At that time, I still felt the effect of my deferred tenure-track status. Maybe some of the mistreatment that I experienced as an adjunct and non-tenure track lecturer was intended to prepare me to be able to lead an entire team of faculty with compassion, integrity, and virtue. Perhaps my commitment to excellence in teaching, research, service, and citizenship would make me a better candidate for dean than others. Maybe even all of the administrative experience that I gained in my previous appointments prepared me for such an opportunity. Was I too young to begin considering a deanship role, or to be considered for one? Did I possess the experience, skills, and knowledge to be an effective dean? Did I need to become a department head or chair before becoming a dean? I pondered over these questions and later arrived at the fact that in my heart of hearts I truly desired to become the dean of a business school.

David McClelland's Theory of Needs helped me to understand where I was mentally as I assessed whether I should apply for the position. McClelland profoundly composed the theory that high achievers have needs that ascend from the level of achievement to affiliation and finally to the level of power. I needed the institutional power to lead changes that would be beneficial for students, faculty, and a host of internal and external stakeholder groups. I did decide to apply. However that particular time or place wasn't the right fit for me. I applied for several other Business School Dean positions at other institutions, but to no avail.

But while I was in the application queues, God gave me a vision in my sleep that was an absolute call for action. This calling temporarily interrupted the vitality of my deanship ambitions.

"Go to Michigan and build!"

Now what, when, and why does God want me to do that, I thought to myself. Build what? Were we to continue building our careers, a ministry, a foundation, a new home? Why Michigan? I grew up there. Why did I need to return there? We were living comfortably in the Chicago-land area. God blessed us to purchase our dream home, which sat on an acre of land in a nice suburb What could be better? I was mentally thrown by this change of direction. Moreover, I was determined to try to make sense out of the instructions and to convince Nicole that these were indeed God's directions and not my own. As time went on, we both began to realize that the direction that God ordained wasn't a figment of our imaginations, but it was truly a divine order to act. There was a sequence of events that followed the dream that provided a greater affirmation of what was to come.

Surprisingly, I was notified on what would've been Mom's 62nd birthday that I had been nominated and named the 2011 GMI/Kettering University Distinguished Alumni of Civic Achievement. I had to rejoice in the fact that I was named a Distinguished Alumni at the same university that I once flunked out of.

As we traveled to Kettering University and took in the festivities of alumni weekend, I could only imagine what it would be like to live in Michigan again. After I delivered my award acceptance speech, the Department Head of Industrial Engineering and Business approached our table. He informed me that in couple of years Kettering would conduct a national search for a new business professor. He asked if I would be interested, and if I would consider applying for the position, when and if it became available. I knew that Kettering University didn't have any dean positions in its organizational structure, but in my response I was still mindful of God's directions. "Of course I am interested and will definitely apply as soon as the position becomes available", I responded. I felt chills and goose-bumps all over my body.

Could it be possible that I would someday teach at the same university that I flunked out of? Would I have the opportunity to take part in academically preparing a whole new generation of engineers, technicians, scientists and managers? Could this move be a precursor to someday becoming a business school dean? I didn't have any definitive, summative answers to any of those questions. I decided to apply faith, patience, and obedience to that entire situation and to continue to follow the path that God had ordained. I believed that more raining coins awaited me on this path.

2012-2013 – The Foundation was born

The coins that I dreamed about that aligned my path when I continued to walk in faith were not just for me. I truly believe that each of us was designed to be a blessing to each other. Everything that God has created yields and gives. Consider every living creature. Every earthly creature has the ability to reproduce and to give live. The sun gives us light and energy. The waterways provide a means to travel, nourishment, and cleanliness. I concluded, as humans, we must have the overarching ability under God to yield and to give.

In 2012, we established Dr. C Moorer & Associates, Inc., as a 501(c)3 not-for-profit organization.

Initially, my primary goal for this foundation was to give hope and financial resources to students and educators. However, as I worked to recruit board members and the executive team, our mission and vision began to evolve. Today our mission is to encourage, motivate, and inspire students and educators to reach great promise which results in improved, global citizenship. Our vision is to serve as a global change agency which positively impacts everyone within our span of influence. We believe that every child on every continent has the right to a promising future. These are our core values:

Diversity

Respect

Integrity

Virtue

Excellence

Nobility

We are certainly a "DRIVEN" board and executive team, who seeks to fulfill our purpose and vision, in part by offering several scholarship and grant programs, facilitating a virtual mentoring suite, and performing random acts of kindness. Our goals to build a community learning center in Michigan and to move forward with the Humanity Agenda efforts will be realized in coming years.

Photo Caption: (from left to right) Mrs. Nicole Willis-Moorer, Dr.
Al Rosenbloom, Dr. Jay Jiwani, Dr. Marsha Phelps, Mr. Pete
DePaz, Mrs. Ning Zou, and Mr. Rodney Allen.

The board and executive team are certainly like a family to Nicole and
me. The board challenges us to find and to develop new funding sources
and ways to reach our goals. Not only do they share insights with us, but
they give time, energy, skill and financial resources to ensure that we are
solvent and sound.

One of our biggest professional achievements as an organization is
the development of a library at Dayton Horizon Science Academy
(HSA-Elementary) in Dayton, OH. Dayton (HSA) was the first
recipient of the From Failure to Promise k-12 Educator's Grant. The
grant proposal submitted by the school's director requested assistance in
developing a library for the school. Nicole and I traveled to visit the
school and found that it did not have a library. Teachers kept classroom
reading materials in their classrooms for in-class use only. The teachers
purchased their own reading materials for their students. A school
without a library is akin to a restroom without a door, in my opinion.

We had to act! We collected and purchased school-age appropriate books, reading materials, laptops, and provided a cash stipend to the school's director. On March 8, 2013, the library was officially opened and dedicated as the "Dorris Jean Moorer Memorial Library".

Now the 175 k-5 students at Dayton (HSA-Elementary) in Dayton, OH have thousands of materials to read, explore, and to learn from. They have hope for a better tomorrow and are one step closer to achieving their full potential and promise. This is just one example that

illustrates the type of impact that I envision our foundation having on multiple stakeholder groups. The joy that I felt from seeing the smiles on these children's faces was indescribable. Also to know on that day, as a son, I was able to keep and to fulfill a promise that I made to my dying mother, just two years prior. This will always be an invaluable mental, spiritual, and emotional construct in my mind. This project began in 2012 and was earmarked to be completed in 2013. We were still able to provide (4) other From Failure to Promise k-12 educator's grants that year.

I refused to come down off of the high that altruism provides to those who are fortunate to be able to experience giving. Have you ever given something to a complete stranger that was of value to you? If not, then I encourage you to do so frequently. If you have done so, did you realize that the gesture of giving wasn't really for that person; it was for you? I needed to give hope to those children at that particular time in my life. Sure, perhaps someone else or some other organization would have come along to do so. But I am so honored that God chose us to do it. The spirit and smile of Mrs. Dorris Jean Moorer is now known and recognized posthumously. I committed to giving and sharing far before the thought of a dedication to my mother was even plausible. I advise that we shouldn't give to receive. Give to give, and God will ensure that you will receive.

The momentum from my recent promotion to Associate Professor at Dominican University coupled with the opening of Mother's Library carried me right into my interview at Kettering University. How surreal was this? It was very surreal. *"So, why Michigan and why would you come back to Kettering…most people would give their right hand to have a great position and to work in the Chicago-land area…and you'd come back to Flint, MI?"* These were the types of questions that some of the search committee members asked. I responded to all of these questions confidently and with the knowledge that I was doing exactly what God instructed me to do. I was able to share with the search committee my teaching philosophy, research interests, and most recent accomplishments at Dominican University.

As the interview process went on, I became more and more comfortable with the idea of actually leaving Dominican. The Dominican University School of Business was well on its way to earning the Advancement for the Association of Collegiate Schools of Business (AACSB) accreditation. I kept my vow to help make the Brennan School of Business one of the best business schools in the world. Most significantly, I remained true to my own personal work ethic and standards; which I have adequately named the *PIP* system. I shared with the committee that I've always taken professional pride in exhibiting high amounts of: *Presence, Impact,* and *Performance.* I had a wonderful time on campus and anticipated the final results from the conclusion of the interview process on their end.

Nicole and I placed our home on the market a few months prior to my formal interview at Kettering. We actually secured a lease on a new property in Michigan prior to Kettering extending me a formal offer. We were moving by faith and not by sight. I was offered the position several weeks later. However, the provost wasn't willing to honor my promotion to Associate Professor at Dominican, nor was he willing to give me any credit on the tenure-track clock at Kettering.

February 18, 2013

Mr. Cleamon Moorer

Dear Clem:

   You have met all the appropriate criteria for promotion to the rank of Associate Professor. Therefore, I am pleased to inform you that the Committee on Faculty Appointments has approved your application, effective for the 2013-2014 academic year. My sincere congratulations!

   Clem, the committee commends you on the effectiveness of your teaching and your solid research agenda — having published two peer-reviewed journal articles within the last two years. Your recent appointment to the Academic IT Committee also was noted.

   Keep up the good work. I look forward to your continuing contribution as a member of the Dominican University faculty.

Sincerely,

Donna M. Carroll
President

c. Cheryl Johnson-Odim
    Arvid Johnson

So, assuming the role of an Assistant Professor and starting all over again on the tenure-track clock appeared to be a demotion of sorts. I tried to negotiate. I was bringing 10+ years of classroom, research, and administrative experience to the table. He took a *"take-it or leave it"* stance to my arguments.

What would you have done? Would it have seemed to you that for every step forward that you took you got knocked back three or four steps? What would I have missed that was so great ahead of me if I had of said, "No, this is unreasonable..."? What about the invaluable joy and personal triumph of going From Failure to Promise: "360 Degrees"? I had already taken an uncommon, but successful path to professoriate. To have flunked-out of a prominent institution and to be able to return to that very same institution as a university professor is an unbelievable accomplishment. I perceived that taking that opportunity would be the capstone to my evolution. It wasn't just about me, Nicole, and the boys. Did the people of Detroit and Flint need a good news story to inspire them to stay driven and to continue to strive to reach their full potential and promise? Besides all of that, most importantly…"God himself told me to go to Michigan and to build."

I accepted the position of Assistant Professor. We relocated to Michigan during the summer of 2013. In my heart I knew I was an Associate Professor and even Dean's material for that matter, but I took the demotion anyhow, because my future and realizing my full promise was contingent upon my obedience to God.

I returned to my alma-mater as a peer to professors, who in 1995 had to submit "F" grades to the registrar's office on my behalf. I taught in some of the same classrooms that I once struggled to grasp subject and course concepts in. I was able to share research ideas and pedagogical models with my mentors and former professors. In the classroom, I was able to realize the full promise of the *"my mentor was me"* concept that I developed earlier that year. I was able to reach my students and to let them know that I truly was once in their shoes, and they could someday be like me, and even be much greater than what I could only dream of becoming.

I was back and hungry to teach, eager to reach, driven to serve in the community, and destined to lead. I had gone "360 Degrees" in every respect.

I was appreciative and honored to be in a position to give back to an institution that gave so much to me. This was my 3rd go-round at Kettering University. I was determined to educate students in the areas of international business, management, and strategy but with an emphasis on ethics, virtue, character, and integrity. This generation of engineers and managers needs to take a quadruple-bottom line approach to decision making, which requires an emphasis on *Purpose – People – Planet –* and lastly – *Profits*. The success that I had teaching and reaching students in the classroom is difficult to describe.

There was never a dull moment in the classroom during my first two terms – (summer and fall) of the 2013-2014 academic-year. I continued to conduct my academic research outside of the classroom and I engaged in and led several civic activities in the mid-Michigan area. What more could I ask for?

Well, I wanted to lead, assist, and help the business department to be as strong and notable as the university's award-winning engineering programs. I believed that the potential was there for us to do so much more in the areas of expansion, diversification of programs, quality, and civic engagement. Perhaps you can imagine that some of my paradigm-shifting proposals and suggestions made our department meetings interesting, with a pinch of frustration. Some, but not all of my colleagues suffered from tremendous cases of inertia and the *"this is the way we've always done it…"* mentality. Perhaps some of them felt as though I was coming off as a hot-shot. Be that as it may, my intention was and is always to approach every professional exchange with tact, diplomacy, and objectivity. I couldn't find any valid reasons for the business department to be one of the smallest departments on campus. We prided ourselves on having the biggest *"minor"* on campus. That wasn't good enough of a showing for me. Colleges, universities, schools, and academic departments can't be complacent. As academics, we need to develop and foster exemplary academic programming that prepares students to meet the global challenges of the 21st century.

How could the move back to Kettering not be a good fit after all? I understood that no place would be perfect. I also knew that change takes time; but in most cases, in order for change to happen, there must be a recognized desire or need to change. I was frustrated by not having the commitment from key internal stakeholders to improve the business department, or at the very least help it to return to the type of department that I graduated from. Metaphorically, I felt like I was being buried alive with one tablespoon of sand at a time. But if it was God's will for me to stay at Kettering for the rest of working days, then I was willing to do so. Was the Kettering appointment a bridge to something else? Obviously, I still had a burning desire to lead a School of Business.

I promise that I don't want From Failure to Promise to ever be perceived by anyone as a fairy-tale or at times cliché. The timing and sequence of certain events in my life have been more than ironic. In fact, many sequences have been symbolic of a divine order, or at the very least arranged to enable me to see a bigger picture or pattern. Have you also observed a certain pattern of events in your life that was more than difficult to explain or decipher? At a very basic level, someone may have explained it to you in the simplest terms, "...everything happens for a reason." That conclusion isn't philosophically strong or sound enough. is it? Ghee, thanks Dr. Phil. Many of us want to crack the code, so that we can make more sense out of life and perhaps predict what is to come years down the road.

Anyhow, on September 2nd, which is my birthday, I stumbled across a job posting for a Dean of the School of Business position at Madonna University in Livonia, MI. They were conducting a national search for a business school dean. Could it be possible that I would indeed be the next Dean of the Madonna University School of Business? I applied, because in my heart of hearts I felt that it was the right fit, the right time, and the right place for me and only me.

I was very familiar with Madonna University, because in 1998, I visited Madonna University's School of Business to pick up some information about their graduate degree programs before I knew that I would be relocating to Chicago. I was very impressed and I certainly would've applied for admission into their MBA program after completing my undergraduate degree at Kettering. Nevertheless, I attended Benedictine University instead. Could my academic preparation at Benedictine University coupled with my teaching and administrative duties at Saint Xavier University and Dominican University be the primer that I needed to be a dean at another similar, faith-based institution? Was all of this a mere coincidence? When I sat out to attend Benedictine University back in 2000, I had no idea that the ethos of Catholic Higher Education would eventually be my niche. It is now obvious that God knew and He had a divine plan all along.

2014 – The Harvest

I expressed earlier in this memoir that God will not tease you. He will show you your heart's desire and provide you with the means to receive it. I had to put my own words, faith and understanding back into action again. I didn't realize that there was so much more in store in this "360 Degrees" process. In early 2014, the fruits of my obedience and faith started to rain down in a more than unexpected manner. There are four more events that I would like to share with you as I bring the story of From Failure to Promise: 360 Degrees to a close. It is my hope that these four monolithic events will help you to fully understand that not only will you achieve the desires of your heart, but you can exceed them in order to arrive at your full promise and destiny.

(1) The Benedictine University Alumni Association nominated and named me a 2014 Who's Who *Rising Star.* Yes, another distinguished alumni award, but from an institution where I failed to be admitted into their PhD program.

(2) I also was nominated to be a 2014 Crain's Detroit Business,"Top 40 under 40" business leader. Yes, in the same town, where at times my parents struggled to run a business. I have been featured in news articles which have provided me the opportunity to make mention of C&M Collision, and its overall contribution to my present-day success. How dichotomous could one's journey be? Had it not been for my troubling and humble beginnings, would I have the same appreciation for what is transpiring at this point? When I began my journey with hope, I only hoped to do well enough to take care of myself and perhaps a family at some point. God has now blessed me with a platform, voice, and skillset to work to help to address the global woes of genocide, educational inadequacies, and hopelessness.

> *But when you give to the needy, do not let your left hand know what your right hand is doing, so that your giving may be in secret. Then your Father, who sees what is done in secret, will reward you.*
>
> — Matthew 6: 3-4

God is and has certainly rewarded me openly. He can and will do even more for you! I will always continue to glorify His name in all that I do. I learned earlier to glorify God and praise Him for the work that He has done for and in the lives of others. One of my personal heroes is a shining example of the impact that I hope to someday have on the lives of others. Dr. Ben Carson is a "giver" of hope, love, compassion, and understanding to so many. He is also a tremendous benefactor to thousands of children and schools all around the country. Would I ever be able to meet and have a conversation with my childhood hero?

Dr. Cleamon Moorer, Dr. Ben Carson, and Mrs. Nicole Willis-Moorer (left to right) April 12, 2014

(3) Of course I would. As I chatted with inarguably the greatest, pediatric neurosurgeon to ever live, my mind drifted for a moment back to the days when I only hoped for such a time as that one. But it did actually come to pass. That was the moment! God granted me the opportunity to simply thank Dr. Carson for being an inspiration and for having an indelible impact on me at a very pivotal point in my life. Dr. Carson embraced Nicole and I and he demonstrated for us just how important it is to be gracious, humble, and engaging with all people, from all walks of life. What an outstanding human being, I thought to myself as I listened to him speak and address the crowd. He and his wife, Mrs. Candy Carson are exemplary role models and Nicole and I are forever fortunate for having the opportunity to meet them.

I began to realize that this series of events was a part of a harvest season of sorts that I envisioned several years prior. It was amazing to me that I could shout and cry tears of joy during this period at the same magnitude that I shouted and cried tears of sorrow during some of my most trying moments. The pendulum does shift. Trouble can't and will not last always. I now know that I have the resolve to go from one extreme to the next and still keep the faith, while encouraging others to do the same, regardless of the circumstances.

"give thanks in all circumstances; for this is God's will for you in Christ Jesus"

1 Thessalonians 5:18

(4) I was notified in April that I was a finalist in the national search for the next dean of Madonna University's School of Business following a very thorough, initial screening process. I prepared and successfully demonstrated to the search committee and the campus community my vision for 21st century business education. I was able to demonstrate my commitment, passion, energy, potential to lead, and necessary skill-sets for guiding the School of Business to higher heights. I was offered and accepted the position of Dean of the School of Business at Madonna University, approximately two weeks after my campus visit. The vision statement that I've constructed for our business school is as follows:

The Madonna University School of Business aspires to be a leading provider of business education in the Metropolitan Detroit-area and beyond, internationally recognized for preparing students to create, manage, serve, and lead organizations with humanism, ethics and integrity.

I am very proud of the students, faculty, staff and alumni of the Madonna University School of Business. I am honored to be anointed by God and appointed to help to build and rebuild the minds, hearts, and lives of students in this region and beyond. We also offer classes and degree programs in China, Dubai, Haiti, and Online. There is so much more in store for us as we celebrate 40 years of offering quality business education in the Livonia, MI area and beyond.

As a person, and as a professional, God has taken me From Failure to Promise. My uncommon path to professoriate led to a deanship and so much more. I've completely gone "360 Degrees".

If reading this memoir has positively impacted, inspired and influenced you, then my legacy is cemented. God willing, I am not done. There are still seeds of promise, dreams and visions that are deep in my heart. I will continue to work relentlessly to manifest them before my days on earth are complete.

360 degrees represents a full circle. I've come full-circle and am in the process of making my mark on the world. I now challenge you to take a 360-degree view of your life and the role that you can take in leaving the world better than how you found it. I've developed a model, called the "**7 Spheres of Influence and Integration Model**" to illustrate how one person can respond to the epiphany, **"YOU"** can change the world for the better.

Dr. C. Moorer's 7 Spheres of Influence and Integration Model

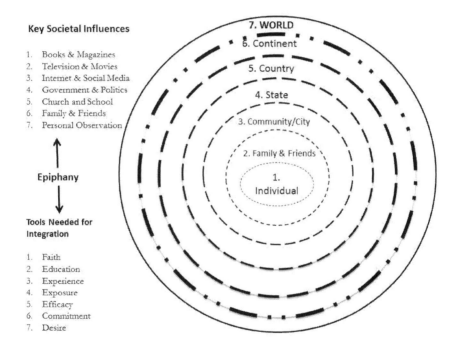

Key Societal Influences

1. Books & Magazines
2. Television & Movies
3. Internet & Social Media
4. Government & Politics
5. Church and School
6. Family & Friends
7. Personal Observation

Epiphany

Tools Needed for Integration

1. Faith
2. Education
3. Experience
4. Exposure
5. Efficacy
6. Commitment
7. Desire

7. WORLD
6. Continent
5. Country
4. State
3. Community/City
2. Family & Friends
1. Individual

Most of us would agree that from our earliest recollection we were told and later realized that we were a part of something or belonged to something or to someone. The homeless and desolate exist in a global society that is filled with all types of people who live in a vast array of situations and circumstances.

I used a set of seven spheres to illustrate the groupings that can help to portray the human relations experience. By nature, we are impacted by and can impact circles one through four (self; family and friends; community; and home state) much easier than circles five through seven. I refer to circles one through three as our immediate circle(s) or comfort zone. We are obviously most familiar and connected to whatever has happened, will happen, or is happening in our immediate circle, comfort zone, or "our world".

However, many of the key societal influences illustrated in the diagram can serve as a means to inform us about issues and events that take place outside of our most immediate circles. How does the information that pertains to others who are outside of your immediate circle(s) affect you?

We live in a world that is plagued by innumerable challenges and issues. Now of course the direct impact that many of these issues have on an individual can be determined by how close they are to the issue. The apathetic...ask, "...so what does that have to do with me?" That's outside of my circle. The empathetic...ask, "how can I help?", or they have a gut-level wish to help others.

The empathetics who respond to the epiphany that they can and must act understand that their existence and legacy rests on helping others. The late Dr. Martin Luther King, Jr. reiterated this point, when he said, *"Life's most persistent and urgent question is: What are you doing for others?"*

If you are empathetic to the plights that many of our world's global citizens face, then please keep reading. For those of you who aren't so empathetic, I also encourage you to bear with me for a little while longer.

A great, global society can only be realized by and through the development of strong, healthy, and successful individuals. There is no exception to this rule. The question becomes what type of epiphany do global change agents experience that equips them with a sense of responsibility to change the world for the better. Dr. Ben Carson, Winston Churchill, Bill Gates, Mahatma Ghandi, Mikhail Gorbachev, Aung San Suu Kyi, Nelson Mandela, Rosa Parks, Desmond Tutu, and a host of other globe-changers realized at some point in their journeys that their purpose was to take a stand to make a difference.

Global change agents interpret the information provided by and through key societal influences somewhat differently than most.

It appears that they view the same information that is available to others as a "call to action". The epiphany or eureka moment that they experience inspires them to garner resources, support, and to utilize their toolkit in an attempt to address the social woes that plague others. They used their faith, education, experience, education, exposure, efficacy, and desire to integrate themselves into circles four through seven, in order to address national and global issues or causes.

Throughout this memoir, I've discussed several issues and causes that are dear to my heart. I will continue to apply every tool in my integration toolkit to address widespread hopelessness, educational inequalities, and genocide. What's your cause? By what does your legacy depend on? Who have you, or who will you, positively impact, inspire and influence to reach great promise that results in improved global citizenship?

It's not by mere happenstance that you've read From Failure to Promise: 360 Degrees. Please go forth to respond to your own personal "call(s) to action".

It's up to you and me to make a difference.

P.S. I will write again in coming years, perhaps as the president of a fine college or university, until then...

I extend you, my most sincere and kindest regards.

Cleamon Moorer, Jr., D.B.A.